THE BEGINNING OF WISDOM

Prayers for Growth and Understanding

edited by
Thomas Becknell and
Mary Ellen Ashcroft

M

Moorings
Nashville, Tennessee
A Division of The Ballantine Publishing Group,
Random House, Inc.

For our children—

Christopher and Jessalyn Becknell
Andrew, Stephen, and Susannah Ashcroft

—who teach us as they grow in learning and faith.

CONTENTS

—Acknowledgments—

We are deeply grateful to more than one hundred men and women, ancient and modern, who in their pursuit of wisdom and understanding, set down their prayers in writing.

We would like to express our thanks to the many students, teachers, colleagues, and friends who made this book possible—especially to:

- Shelly Goodwin, a student whose requests for some of these prayers inspired the idea;
- Laura Jensen for her meticulous research, but most of all for her constant friendship;
- our colleagues—Sue Foster, John Lawyer, Carl Rasmussen, Patricia Beckford, Jim Moline, Richard Peterson, Katherine Nevins, Robert Kistler, Deb Harless, Keith Anderson, Elizabeth Peterson, and Charles Olson—for their wisdom, suggestions, and encouragement;
- the Bethel College Alumni Association for an initial grant;
- Janine McFarland and Michael Martin for assistance in preparing the manuscript.

In working on this book, we inevitably have remembered those teachers who have been instrumental in our learning:

Thanks to Patricia Will for the wonderful gift of music. Thanks to professors Beatrice Batson and Rolland Hein at Wheaton College for inviting me into the amazing world of literature. Thanks to Don Postema and Wayne Roosa from whom I yet may master the fine art of teaching.

Thomas Becknell

Thanks to Mrs. Holzer who fired my enthusiasm for learning at Bellingham High School and to many at The College of St. Catherine (St. Paul, Minn.) who rekindled the flames years later, especially Dr. Bill Myers and Sr. Margery Smith.

Mary Ellen Ashcroft

$\mathcal{I}$NTRODUCTION

In a world of talk-show celebrities, twenty-three-minute solutions to sitcom dilemmas, and instant credit, who wants wisdom? We can hardly relate to Solomon, who chose wisdom—we would have taken the wealth. Or the apostle Paul who prayed that the church be filled with knowledge of God—we would have chosen that the church be filled with good pledging congregants. Wisdom doesn't appeal. We've forgotten that to the Hebrew mind wisdom was eminently practical, helping the wise to distinguish between right and wrong, to follow God's path. We have more often pulled our images of wisdom from Greek thought, where we encounter an otherworldly sage contemplating the mysteries or a clever debater arguing minuscule points with great verbal agility. This doesn't appeal to us, so wisdom has sunk to rock bottom in a contemporary wish list.

Despite wisdom's low ratings, we need it desperately. The beginning of wisdom is our recognition of our need for God, for growth, a need that has governed the men and women who are our parents in the faith. They set an example for us by pursuing wisdom as if it were a matter of life and death.

The men and women whose prayers are represented in this book, some without formal education, some with immense depths of learning, have all pursued wisdom. And all of them pray. Missionary or mystic, teacher or activist, scientist or poet, they teach us here, not through a demonstration of their intellect, but through the example of their prayers. From them we learn the secret of surrounding the journey toward wisdom with prayer.

Most of us know that learning happens in a variety of classrooms—from the volunteer work in a ghetto, to the encounter with a new culture thousands of miles from home, to the Outward Bound ropes course, to the quiet corner of a bedroom where someone opens a book, to the community orchestra where we learn to blend our harmonies with other amateur musicians. And learning happens in more formal settings—in the classrooms of schools and universities, book discussion groups, Sunday school classes, and Bible studies. Growth often catches us in one of these "classrooms."

When we care deeply about things in our lives—our families, our vocations, our countries— we pray about them. And so it should be with our pursuit of wisdom. We bring ourselves, individually or corporately, to God, asking that our learning and growth may be a collaboration with the Source of all wisdom, a cooperative process, as he prepares our minds and hearts. And as we move toward greater understanding, we need prayer— when we struggle with failure (or success), when we encounter feelings of inadequacy and uncertainty, when we long for clarity and focus. We are compelled to pray.

But sometimes words fail us. "Your thoughts don't have words every day," wrote even the articulate poet Emily Dickinson. When we are committing our growth to God, as our minds are being stretched or when our perspective of the world or of ourselves is being shifted, at such times we may feel driven to pray, but struggle to find the words.

The Beginning of Wisdom grew out of our own practical need to find words that would articulate for us, in prayer, the complex thoughts and emotions that seem to accompany almost any experience of learning. What we have found from using these prayers in our own classrooms, with other teachers, with fellow seekers of insight, and in our personal prayer lives is that these are eminently "prayable" prayers—clear, useful, heart-driven expressions of men and women who have prayed well.

These are prayers to encourage you in your pursuit of growth and understanding. The sequence of six chapters is designed to complement the natural process of learning—from prayers of praise and thanksgiving to "the source of wisdom," to the concluding prayers for vision beyond. To those unaccustomed to using written prayers, these expressions can be liberating; freed from the distraction of trying to compose our thoughts, we can use these words to concentrate on the act of prayer itself—an act that usually requires more listening than speaking. We hope that in using them, you'll find prayer becoming a natural part of the whole process of learning—whether in the course of formal learning or in the lifelong experience of learning outside the classroom.

CHAPTER 1

Prayers to the Source of All Wisdom

The story of Solomon's wisdom and how he got it is a familiar one to most Sunday school children. Pleased that the new king Solomon did not ask for wealth, honor, long life, or victory over his ene- mies, God granted his request for wisdom and un- derstanding, giving him not only unparalleled pru- dence, but also unsurpassed wealth and prestige.

The Scriptures persistently urge us to seek wis- dom above wealth. Indeed, wisdom is one of the few commodities we are specifically instructed to ask for: "If any of you is lacking in wisdom," writes James, "ask God, who gives to all generously and ungrudgingly" (James 1:5).

The prayers in this first chapter acknowledge God as the source of all wisdom. Many of these are ancient prayers—from Caedmon, Aquinas, Catherine of Siena, Clement of Alexandria, the apostle Paul, and others. Perhaps those early Christians recognized, more readily than modern believers do, the limits of human wisdom and un- derstanding. "Though I do not know myself," prayed Hilary, a fourth-century Christian, "yet I perceive so much that I marvel at thee the more because I am ignorant of myself." We praise the source of faith and learning, not only because God expects our adoration, but because it preserves us from intellectual arrogance and self-pride—or, as Thomas Troeger puts it, from "the blunder / of believing that our thought / has displaced the grounds for wonder / which the ancient prophets taught."

These prayers to the source of all wisdom provide an essential starting point for those who seek growth and understanding—namely, that wisdom, like prayer itself, begins with God. "The fear of the LORD is the beginning of wisdom" (Proverbs 9:10).

All-Wise God

Eugene Peterson

All-wise God, the world is in confusion and disarray as information accumulates and there is no one to interpret it. Give me, along with all people of faith, wisdom to lead my friends and neighbors to live wisely by the vision you provide in Jesus Christ. Amen.

Eugene Peterson spent more than thirty years as pastor of a Presbyterian church in Maryland. Currently, he is professor of spiritual theology at Regent College, and he is the author of numerous books, including *Praying with the Psalms*, *Praying with Jesus*, and *Praying with the Early Christians*.

The Fountain of All Wisdom

Venerable Bede

I implore you, good Jesus, that as in your mercy you have given me to drink in with delight the words of your knowledge, so of your loving kindness you will also grant me one day to come to you, the fountain of all wisdom, and to stand for ever before your face. Amen.

A historian and monk of the early Middle Ages, Bede (673–735) became known as "venerable" Bede because of his holy life. His book *Ecclesiastical History of the English People* provided a carefully documented record of the development of Christianity in Anglo-Saxon England. This prayer is above his grave in Durham Cathedral.

For Those Who Teach and Those Who Learn

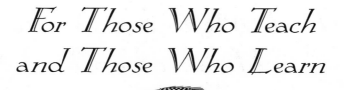

The Book of Common Prayer

Almighty God, the fountain of all wisdom: Enlighten by your Holy Spirit those who teach and those who learn, that, rejoicing in the knowledge of your truth, they may worship you and serve you from generation to generation; through Jesus Christ our Lord, who lives and reigns with you and the Holy Spirit, one God, for ever and ever. Amen.

The Book of Common Prayer, first composed by Thomas Cranmer, archbishop of Canterbury, in 1549, continues to serve as a guide to worship within the Anglican Communion worldwide, including Episcopal churches today.

Teach Me to Know You Here on Earth

Elisabeth Elliot

Lord, you have said, I am the Way—not that we
shall never be confused.
You have said, I am the Truth—not that we shall
have all the answers.
And, I am the Life—not that we shall never die.
Teach me to know you here on earth—
in its tangled maze of pathways, to know you as
the Way; in its unanswerable mysteries, to
know you as the Truth; in the face of suffering
and death, to know you as the Life.
Thank you, Lord, for not offering us a method,
saying, This is the Way.
Thank you for not granting us a set of invariable
propositions, saying, This is the Truth.
Thank you for not delivering us from being
human, saying, This is the Life.
Thank you, Lord, for saying instead, I am, and for
giving us yourself.

Elisabeth Elliot was the wife of Jim Elliot, one of five American
missionaries martyred by Auca Indians in Ecuador in 1956. She
told that story in her book, *Through Gates of Splendor*. Elisabeth
Elliot is the author of a number of other books.

Praise for the Creator's Might

Caedmon

Now must we praise the Warden of Heaven's
   realm
The Creator's might and his mind's thought,
The glorious works of the Father;
How of every wonder
He, the Lord, the eternal, laid the foundation.
He shaped erst, for the sons of men,
Heaven as their roof, Holy Creator,
The middle-world, he, mankind's Warden,
Eternal Lord, afterwards prepared
The earth for men, Lord Almighty.

Known as the earliest Anglo-Saxon Christian poet, Caedmon
(seventh century) was a laborer at the monastery at Whitby (in
what is now North Yorkshire, England) when he was given a vision, after which he was able to compose verse praising God.
He became a monk and is venerated by some as a saint.

The Wisdom and Knowledge of God

The Apostle Paul

O the depth of the riches both of the wisdom and knowledge of God! How unsearchable are his judgments, and his ways past finding out! For who hath known the mind of the Lord? Or who hath been his counselor? Or who hath first given to him, and it shall be recompensed unto him again? For of him, and through him, and to him, are all things: to whom be glory for ever. Amen.

Saul of Tarsus was converted to Christianity on the road to Damascus after persecuting the church. He thereafter became an apostle, planting churches and teaching the new believers in what is now Turkey and Greece. This prayer is taken from his letter to the largely gentile church in Rome, written around A.D. 57.

Great God of All Wisdom

Jane Parker Huber

Great God of all wisdom, of science and art,
O grant us the wisdom that comes from the heart.
Technology, learning, philosophy, youth—
All leave us still yearning for your word of truth.

Where people are starving, where wars devastate,
A future we're carving of anguish and hate.
God, turn us around and invade all our lives
Till justice is found and your righteousness thrives.

Call us to a new day of promise and trust
That outlines a new way of life that is just.
Call us to build bridges, deep chasms to clear,
Mark trails over ridges of bias and fear.

Creator of visions as well as of stars,
O mend our divisions and heal all our scars.
You reign over history, both present and past,
Most challenging mystery from first to the last.

Born in Tsinan, China, Jane Parker Huber was educated at
Northfield School for Girls, Wellesley College, and Hanover
College. Many of her hymns have been composed for the
United Presbyterian Women. She lives in Indianapolis.

O Creator, Shed the Light of Your Wisdom

Thomas Aquinas

O Creator of the universe, who has set the stars in the heavens and causes the sun to rise and set, shed the light of your wisdom into the darkness of my mind. Fill my thoughts with the loving knowledge of you, that I may bring your light to others. Just as you can make even babies speak your truth, instruct my tongue and guide my pen to convey the wonderful glory of the gospel. Make my intellect sharp, my memory clear, and my words eloquent, so that I may faithfully interpret the mysteries which you have revealed.

Thomas Aquinas (1225–74), born at Rullasecca, was related to the emperor and king of France, and was destined by his parents to be abbot of Monte Cassino where he went to school. Because he was determined to join a Dominican order, his family imprisoned him for fifteen months. When he joined the order, he studied, taught, and wrote in several cities. He is best known for his *Summa Theologica*, through which he explored issues of reason and faith.

Enlighten the Darkness of My Heart

Francis of Assisi

O most high, glorious God, enlighten the darkness
   of my heart and give me
     a right faith,
       a certain hope
         and a perfect love, understanding and
           knowledge,
O Lord,
   that I may carry out your holy and true
     command.
Amen.

Many legends have grown up around the life of Francis of Assisi
(1182–1226). Converted to Christianity at age twenty-three, he
lived a life of deliberate poverty. In 1208, he set out on foot to
preach the gospel. Others, inspired by his gentleness and his
service to the poor, formed a religious order, the Franciscans.

A Prayer of Wonder

Richard J. Foster

I glory in your handiwork, O God:
 towering mountains and deep valleys,
 dense forests and expansive deserts,
 fathomless depths of blue below and
  immeasurable
 heights of blue above.

When I peer into the universe of the telescope
and the universe of the microscope I stand in awe
at:
 the complexity and the simplicity,
 the order and the chaos,
 and the infinite variety of colors everywhere.

When I watch the little creatures that creep upon
the earth
I marvel at:
 such purpose,
  such direction,
   such design;
 and yet
  such freedom,
   such openness,
    such creativity.

O Lord God, Creator of the hummingbird and the
Milky Way, I am lost in wonder at your originality.
Amen.

Born in New Mexico and author of several books, including
Prayer: Finding the Heart's True Home and *Celebration of Discipline,* Richard Foster is an ordained minister in the Society of
Friends.

This Complex Tapestry

Clifford Swartz

All things worship thee,
Revealing by their form and actions
The patterns of creation.
This complex tapestry is proper subject
For analysis and praise.
By such study, humans worship their creator,
And fulfill their proper role
Which is the understanding of this world.
The songs of great composers or the whales
Are meaningless without the tutored ear.
The sunsets and cathedrals are diminished
When we are blind to intricate details.
Worship in this highest form must be creative.

But we can praise thee in a simpler way.
The soaring gull caresses rising air,
The dolphins leap in play, and lovers are
    enraptured.
When creatures revel in the joy of life
They also worship their creator.
Perhaps the bursting gladness of this world
Can balance out the cries of anguish.

If we believe that this is so,
And that there is a purpose
In the universal scheme
And in our individual lives,
We also worship thee.

Clifford Swartz is professor of physics at the University of New York, Stony Brook, and author of a number of physics textbooks. He began writing prayers in the choir loft at church.

In You I Believe

from "Misa Campesina"

Firmly I believe, Lord,
that your prodigious mind
created this whole earth.
To your artist's hand
beauty owed its birth:
the stars and the moon,
the cottages, the lakes,
little boats bobbing
down river to the sea,
vast coffee plantations,
white cotton fields
and the forests felled
by the criminal axe. . . .

In you I believe,
maker of thought and music,
maker of the wind,
maker of peace and love.

This prayer is part of the creed from the Nicaraguan Mass called "Misa Campesina." Prayers in the Mass cry out to Christ for solidarity with the oppressed. While the class struggle is present in the liturgy, there are no recriminations or threats. Instead it offers confession and praise and expresses joy as an intrinsic element of choice.

Guidance from the Eternal

Alcuin of York

Eternal light, shine in our hearts.
Eternal goodness, deliver us from evil.
Eternal power, be our support.
Eternal wisdom, scatter the darkness
    of our ignorance.
Eternal pity, have mercy on us,
That with all our heart and mind
    and soul and strength we may seek thy face
    and be brought by thine infinite mercy
    to thy holy presence.

Best known as the inspiration behind the Carolingian Renais-
sance, Alcuin (ca. 735–804) was born and educated in York before being master of the cathedral school there. He became advisor to Charlemagne after meeting him in 781, and set up an
important school and library.

Prayer for Wisdom

Benjamin Franklin

O Powerful Goodness! bountiful Father! merciful Guide! Increase in me that Wisdom which discovers my truest Interests; Strengthen my Resolutions to perform what that Wisdom dictates. Accept my kind Offices to thine other Children, as the only Return in my Power for thy continual Favours to me.

Born in Boston, Benjamin Franklin (1706–90) ran away to Philadelphia when he was seventeen, becoming a printer. He founded the first circulating library in the United States, and served as minister to France and as president of Pennsylvania. In 1771, at the age of sixty-five, Franklin began his famous autobiography in which this prayer appears.

Praise the Source of Faith and Learning

Thomas H. Troeger

Praise the source of faith and learning
who has sparked and stoked the mind
with a passion for discerning
how the world has been designed.
Let the sense of wonder flowing
from the wonders we survey
keep our faith forever growing
and renew our need to pray:

God of wisdom, we acknowledge
that our science and our art
and the breadth of human knowledge
only partial truth impart.
Far beyond our calculation
lies a depth we cannot sound
where your purpose for creation
and the pulse of life are found.

May our faith redeem the blunder
of believing that our thought
has displaced the grounds for wonder
which the ancient prophets taught.
May our learning curb the error
which unthinking faith can breed
lest we justify some terror
with an antiquated creed.

A Presbyterian minister and professor at the Rochester Center
for Theological Studies, Thomas H. Troeger is the author of
such books as *Meditation: Escape to Reality* (1977), *Are You
Saved? Answers to the Awkward Question* (1979), and *Creating
Fresh Images for Preaching* (1982).

As two currents in a river
fight each other's undertow
till converging they deliver
one coherent steady flow,
blend, O God, our faith and learning
till they carve a single course
While they join as one returning
praise and thanks to you their source.

Pied Beauty

Gerard Manley Hopkins

Glory be to God for dappled things—
    For skies of couple-colour as a brinded cow;
        For rose-moles all in stipple upon trout
        that swim;
Fresh-firecoal chestnut-falls; finches' wings;
    Landscapes plotted and pieced—fold, fallow,
    and plough;
        And all trades, their gear and tackle and
        trim.

All things counter, original, spare, strange;
    Whatever is fickle, freckled (who knows how?)
        With swift, slow; sweet, sour; adazzle, dim;
He fathers-forth whose beauty is past change:
        Praise him.

Born near London, Gerard Manley Hopkins (1844–89) at-
tended Oxford and originally planned to become a painter. But
when he joined the Catholic Church at age twenty-two, his
plans changed, and shortly after, he decided to become a Jesuit.
At age forty, he became professor of classics at University College in Dublin, but died of typhoid a few years later. His poetry
was not collected and published until 1918.

O Educator, Father

Clement of Alexandria

O Educator, be gracious to thy children, O Educator, Father, guide of Israel, Son and Father, both
one, Lord. Give to us, who follow thy command,
to fulfill the likeness of thy image, and to see, according to our strength, the God who is both a
good God and a Judge who is not harsh. Do thou
thyself bestow all things on us who dwell in thy
peace, who have been placed in thy city, who sail
the sea of sin unruffled, that we may be made tran-
quil and supported by the Holy Spirit, the unutterable Wisdom, by night and day, unto the perfect
day, to sing eternal thanksgiving to the one only
Father and Son, Son and Father, Educator and
Teacher with the Holy Spirit. All things are for
the One, in whom are all things, through whom
eternity is, of whom all men are members, to
whom is glory, and the ages, whose are all things
in their goodness; all things, in their beauty; all
things, in their wisdom; all things, in their justice.
To him be glory now and forever. Amen.

Clement of Alexandria (ca. 150–215) was a theologian, probably an Athenian by birth. Forced to leave his homeland by persecution in 202, he tried to bring the best of Greek philosophy
to bear on Christian theology. He taught that Christ, the Logos,
was both interpreter of God to humanity and the source of all
human reason. He was martyred around 215.

You, Eternal Truth

Catherine of Siena

You, O Eternal Trinity, are a deep sea, into which the more I enter, the more I find, and the more I find, the more I seek. The soul cannot be satisfied in your abyss, for she continually hungers after you, the Eternal Trinity, desiring to see you with the light of your light.

As the hart desires the springs of living water, so my soul desires to leave the prison of this dark body and see you in truth.

O abyss, O Eternal Godhead, O sea profound, what more could you give me than yourself? You are the fire that ever burns without being consumed; you consume in your heat all the soul's self-love; you are the fire which takes away cold; with your light you illuminate me so that I may know all your truth. Clothe me, clothe me with yourself, Eternal Truth, so that I may run this mortal life with true obedience, and with light of your most holy faith.

As a young woman, Catherine Benincasa of Siena (1347–80) once cut off her hair to discourage suitors. In time she became a Dominican nun, known for her service to the poor and sick and her conversion of sinners. She eventually became a highly sought spiritual authority. She never learned to write, but dictated her letters and a book.

With Christ in the School of Prayer

Andrew Murray

O my blessed Lord Jesus, teach me to understand Your lesson, that it is the indwelling Spirit, streaming from You, uniting to You, who is the Spirit of prayer. Teach me what it is as an empty, wholly consecrated vessel, to yield myself to His being my life. Teach me to honor and trust Him, as a living person, to lead my life and my prayer. Teach me especially in prayer to wait in holy silence, and give Him place to breathe within me His unutterable intercession. And teach me that through Him it is possible to pray without ceasing, and to pray without failing, because He makes me partaker of the never-ceasing and never-failing intercession in which You, the Son, appear before the Father.

Born in South Africa in 1828, Andrew Murray studied theology in Europe. He served in a number of Dutch Reformed Churches in the Orange Free State and the Cape Colony. He is best remembered for his many devotional books, especially his books on deepening the spiritual life, such as *Like Christ*, *With Christ in the School of Prayer*, and *Holy in Christ*.

CHAPTER 2

Prayers to Prepare
the Heart and Mind

Often the most difficult part of a learning experience is the preparation. Sometimes we simply cannot find the time to open a book, to prepare the
lesson, or even think; the press of other duties or
the call of other voices keep us from it. Sometimes
we struggle with discouragement or weariness or
lack of confidence. And sometimes the terror of
the blank page, or the tediousness of the research,
or the complexity of a problem overwhelms us.

These prayers show us how to ask for God's
help in facing the challenges of learning. They are
remarkably clear, practical expressions that can as-
sist us in sorting through the muddled thoughts
and emotions we may feel at such times.

Some of these prayers will encourage us to
name specifically the barriers and distractions we
confront. Mechthild of Magdeburg prays simply,
"Please, wake me up." W. E. B. Du Bois sees the
barrier of procrastination and prays for help in
learning that "today . . . our best studying can be
done and not some future day or future year."
Sarah Klos is concerned about the worry and in-
difference and frenzy in her classroom. Theodore
Roethke, in his "Prayer before Study," asks for de-

liverance from the self-centeredness that he finds so constricting. And a "Prayer from Kenya" confesses that our own cowardice, laziness, and arrogance get in the way of understanding.

Certain prayers also help us to appreciate the complexity of the learning process, and to ask for God's guidance and direction. "Broaden our ideas," prays Origen; and some of these prayers will indeed stretch us. Susanna Wesley, for example, explains that all of her intellectual, philosophical, and rhetorical skills will mean nothing to her if she does not also acquire a heart-driven, *experiential* knowledge of God. John Calvin reminds us that the mind, the memory, the heart, and the understanding must all be integrated with God's help. Believing, then, that the spiritual life and the intellectual life are thoroughly integrated, Herbert Brokering can pray, "Come to me in my mind, Jesus," and Oswald Chambers can ask, "Lord, interpret Yourself to me."

Above all, we learn to be direct and straightforward in our requests for God's guidance. These individuals do not beat around the bush in their prayers; they say exactly what they need: "invigorate my studies, and direct my inquiries"; "strengthen my memory"; "teach me to listen"; "bestow upon us the meaning of words"; "help me really to get into things." Praying such prayers will prepare our hearts and enable us to take our minds off our insecurities and other outside distractions, to remain attentive and receptive, and to focus confidently upon the task before us.

Prayer from Kenya

From the cowardice that dares not face new truth
From the laziness that is contented with half-truth
From the arrogance that thinks it knows all truth,
Good Lord, deliver me.

The church in Africa is said to be the fastest growing in the world; and this prayer, although anonymous, expresses some of the clear-sighted courage and perspective of many African Christians.

Prayers before Study

Samuel Johnson

Almighty God, our heavenly Father, without whose help labor is useless, without whose light search is vain, invigorate my studies, and direct my inquiries, that I may, by due diligence and right discernment, establish myself and others in your holy faith. Take not, O Lord, your Holy Spirit from me; let not evil thoughts have dominion in my mind. Let me not linger in ignorance, but enlighten and support me, for the sake of Jesus Christ our Lord. Amen.

Almighty God, the Giver of Wisdom, without whose help resolutions are vain, without whose blessing study is ineffectual, enable me, if it be thy will, to attain such knowledge as may qualify me to direct the doubtful, and instruct the ignorant, to prevent wrongs, and terminate contentions; and grant that I may use that knowledge which I shall attain, to your glory and my own salvation, for Jesus Christ's sake. Amen.

Known as an author, lexicographer, and conversationalist, Samuel Johnson (1709–84) was also known for his high church piety in the eighteenth-century Church of England. He was generous with the pen and faithful in his religious duties.

Christ Our Teacher

Janet Morley

Christ our teacher,
you reach into our lives
not through instruction, but story.
Open our hearts to be attentive;
that seeing, we may perceive,
and hearing, we may understand,
and understanding, may act upon your word,
in your name. Amen.

Janet Morley is adult education advisor for the relief organization Christian Aid. She has been active in the Movement for
the Ordination of Women in the Anglican Church in the
United Kingdom. She is also a contributor to, and coeditor of,
the worship anthology *Celebrating Women*.

Teach Us, O God, That Now Is the Time

W. E. B. Du Bois

Teach us, O God, that now is the accepted time—not tomorrow, not some more convenient season. It is today that our best studying can be done and not some future day or future year. It is today that we fit ourselves for the greater usefulness of tomorrow. Today is the seed time, now are the hours of work and tomorrow comes the harvest and the play-time. May we learn in youth, when the evil days come not, that the man who plays and then works, rests and then studies, fails and then rushes, is not simply reversing nature, he is missing opportunities and losing the training and preparation which makes work and study and endeavor the touchstone of success.
(Isaiah 49:8-11)

W. E. B. Du Bois (1868–1963), an African American sociologist best known for his book, *The Souls of Black Folk* (1903), opposed the positions of racial compromise and acceptance espoused by Booker T. Washington. The work of Du Bois significantly influenced the thinking of other twentieth-century writers such as Ralph Ellison, Malcolm X, and Toni Morrison.

Lord, Interpret Yourself to Me

Oswald Chambers

O Lord, this morning disperse every mist, and shine clear and strong and invigoratingly. Forgive my tardiness, it takes me so long to awaken to some things. Lord God Omniscient, give me wisdom this day to worship and work aright and be well-pleasing to You. Lord, interpret Yourself to me more and more in fullness and beauty.

Oswald Chambers was born in Aberdeen, Scotland, in 1874. During his lifetime he was principal of the Bible Training School at Clapham, England, and superintendent of the YMCA Camp at Zeitoun, Egypt. His best-known book is *My Utmost for His Highest*, a devotional classic. He died in 1917.

Morning Prayer

Elaine Sommers Rich

Lord, Thou art the water of life.
As this day begins, I am an empty pitcher before
   Thee.
Fill me, O Lord.

Thou art the light of the world.
As this day begins, I am an unlit candle.
Thy light can never shine through me to others
   unless
Thou dost shine in my heart.
Thou art the true light that lightest everyone
That cometh into the world.
Light me, O Lord.

Thou art the true vine.
Unless I dwell in Thee this day,
I can bring forth no fruit.
My leaves turn brown, shrivel, blow away and I
   die.
Let Thy life always flow into me, Thy branch, O
   Lord.

Elaine Sommers Rich is a free-lance writer and teacher now living in Bluffton, Ohio. She and her husband, Dr. Ronald Rich,
spent ten years at the International Christian University in
Tokyo. She is a longtime columnist for the *Mennonite Weekly
Review* and author of *Prayers for Everyday*.

Please, Wake Me Up

Mechthild of Magdeburg

O sweet and loving God,
When I stay asleep too long,
Oblivious to all your many blessings,
Then, please, wake me up,
And sing to me your joyful song.
It is a song without noise or notes.
It is a song of love beyond words,
Of faith beyond the power of human telling.
I can hear it in my soul,
When you awaken me to your presence.

Unhappy with the lack of humiliation in her noble family in
Saxony, Mechthild of Magdeburg (ca. 1210–80) fled to become
a Beguine at Magdeburg, a lay sister who lived in a religious
community not bound by vows. She led a life of penance and
prayer, and her visions of God, published as *The Light of Godhead*, deeply influenced German medieval spirituality.

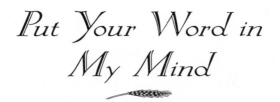

Put Your Word in My Mind

Jacob Boehme

Rule over me this day, O God, leading me on the path of righteousness. Put your Word in my mind and your Truth in my heart, that this day I neither think nor feel anything except what is good and honest. Protect me from all lies and falsehood, helping me to discern deception wherever I meet it. Let my eyes always look straight ahead on the road you wish me to tread, that I might not be tempted by any distraction. And make my eyes pure, that no false desires may be awakened within me.

Jacob Boehme (1575–1624) was first a shepherd and then a shoemaker in Germany. After his first work based on his visions of God was published, he was ordered to stop writing by the Lutheran Church. Boehme continued to write devotional books, which had far-reaching influence on thinkers as disparate as the German romantics such as Hegel, Schelling, and Isaac Newton.

Teach Me to Pray

Henri J. M. Nouwen

Every day I see again that only you can teach me to pray, only you can set my heart at rest, only you can let me dwell in your presence. No book, no idea, no concept or theory will ever bring me close to you unless you yourself are the one who lets these instruments become the way to you.

But Lord, let me at least remain open to your initiative; let me wait patiently and attentively for that hour when you will come and break through all the walls I have erected. Teach me, O Lord, to pray. Amen.

Born in the Netherlands, Henri Nouwen is a priest, a professor, and the author of such books as *The Genesee Diary*, *The Wounded Healer*, *The Road to Daybreak*, and *Creative Ministry*. He has taught at the University of Notre Dame, Yale Divinity School, and Harvard Divinity School. His autobiographical and meditative writings are regarded as among the most spiritually inspirational works of our time.

Let Us Pause from Thinking

Michael Leunig

Let us pray for wisdom. Let us pause from thinking and empty our mind. Let us stop the noise. In the silence let us listen to our heart. The heart which is buried alive. Let us be still and wait and listen carefully. A sound from the deep, from below. A faint cry. A weak tapping. Distant muffled feelings from within. The cry for help.

We shall nurse it and listen respectfully to its story. The heart's story of pain and suffocation, of darkness and yearning. We shall help our feelings to live in the sun. Together again we shall find re-lief and joy.

Michael Leunig is well known in Melbourne, Australia, where his cartoons appear regularly in *The Age*. His prayers are also regularly published and have been collected in *A Common Prayer*. Leunig writes this about his move into writing prayers: "Prayer as a creative lacuna, as an ancient free form and as a marvellous, stabilizing idea, intrigued me greatly. The spirit of the times, so constricted by fashion anxiety, so repressed by ego and scientific authority, seemed the ideal climate for the culti-vation of public prayers."

Give Me
the Listening Ear

Howard Thurman

Give me the listening ear. I seek this day the disciplined mind, the disciplined heart, the disciplined life that makes my ear the focus of attention through which I may become mindful of expressions of life foreign to my own. I seek the stimulation that lifts me out of old ruts and established habits which keep me conscious of my self, my needs, my personal interests.

Give me this day—the eye that is willing to see the meaning of the ordinary, the familiar, the commonplace—the eye that is willing to see my own faults for what they are—the eye that is willing to see the likable qualities in those I may not like—the mistake in what I thought was correct—the strength in what I had labeled as weakness. Give me the eye that is willing to see that you have not left yourself without a witness in every living thing. Thus to walk with reverence and sensitivity through all the days of my life.

Give me the listening ear.
The eye that is willing to see.

Raised by his grandmother, a former slave, Howard Thurman (1900–81) became a Baptist minister and a leader in the civil rights movements of the 1950s and 1960s. He was the first African American to receive a full-time faculty appointment at Boston University. He authored more than twenty books on religion and race, including *Deep River: An Interpretation of Negro Spirituals*, *The Creative Encounter*, and *Apostles of Sensitiveness*.

Prayers for Understanding

John Calvin

May the Lord grant that we may engage in contemplating the mysteries of his heavenly wisdom with really increasing devotion, to his glory and to our edification. Amen.

O Lord, who is the fountain of all wisdom and learning, you have given me the years of my youth to learn the arts and skills necessary for an honest and holy life. Enlighten my mind, that I may acquire knowledge. Strengthen my memory, that I may retain what I have learnt. Govern my heart, that I may always be eager and diligent in my studies. And let your Spirit of truth, judgement and prudence guide my understanding, that I may perceive how everything I learn fits into your holy plan for the world.

Swiss theologian John Calvin (1509–64) was a driving force for the Protestant Reformation in Europe. His Institutes of the Christian Religion (1536) established the foundation for the Reformed tradition within Protestantism. Calvin would often begin his lectures in Geneva with the first of these two prayers.

Prayer before Study

Theodore Roethke

Constricted by my tortured thought,
I am too centered on this spot.

So caged and cadged, so close within
A coat of unessential skin,

I would put off myself and flee
My inaccessibility.

A fool can play at being solemn
Revolving on his spinal column.

Deliver me, O Lord, from all
Activity centripetal.

Educated at the University of Michigan, Theodore Roethke
(1908–63) received numerous awards for his poetry, including
the Pulitzer Prize, Bollingen Prize, and the National Book
Award. Writing to fellow poet John Ciardi, in 1950, Roethke
said, "I believe that to go forward as a spiritual man, it is necessary to go back."

Help Me to Concentrate

Michael Hollings and Etta Gullick

Lord, help me to concentrate on the work that I
am about to do. Don't let me fritter my time away
with idle thoughts, and help me really to get into
things instead of just learning superficially. Keep
my mind open to the thoughts of others, no matter how different from my own. You understand
everything, everybody, and listen to everything.
Help me to be open, more like you; make my understanding and sympathy more like yours.

Michael Hollings is a parish priest in Middlesex, England. He
served for a number of years as a chaplain to Roman Catholic
students at Oxford University. Etta Gullick teaches history and
geographical discovery at Oxford, and spirituality at St.
Stephen's House, an Anglican theological college.

For True Knowledge

Susanna Wesley

Almighty God, I have found that to know Thee
only as a philosopher; to have the most sublime
and curious speculations concerning Thine
essence, Thine attributes, Thy providence; to be
able to demonstrate Thy being from all or any of
the works of nature and to discourse with the
greatest elegancy and propriety of words of Thine
existence or operations, will avail me nothing, unless at the same time I know Thee experimentally:
unless my heart perceive and know Thee to be its
supreme good, its only happiness; unless my soul
feel and acknowledge that she can find no repose,
no peace, no joy, but in loving and being beloved
by Thee; and does accordingly rest in Thee as the
center of her being, the fountain of her pleasure,
the origin of all virtue and goodness, her light, her
life, her strength, her all; everything she wants or
wishes in this world and forever.

Thus let me ever know Thee, O God! I neither
despise nor neglect the light of reason, nor that
knowledge of Thee that may be collected from
this goodly system of created things, but this spec-
ulative knowledge is not the knowledge I want
and wish for above all other. Teach me Thy way,
O Lord! Amen.

Born in London to a famous nonconformist pastor, Susanna
Wesley (1669–1742) decided on her own theological grounds to
join the Church of England. She wrote many letters of guidance, to her family and to other Christians, including her sons,
John and Charles Wesley, the founders of Methodism. Married
to a pastor, she started a popular and controversial "cell group"
in the parsonage at Epworth.

Prayer before Class Begins

Sarah Klos

O Lord, our class is about to begin. Some of us are out of breath. Some of us are worried about all the things we left at home to do. And some of us couldn't care less—about the work we left at home or the work we have to do here in this class.

Slow us down, Lord. Ease the rush of our thoughts. Put our minds on you. Make us stop and think why we are here.

Do you ever speak to us through our parents, friends, our pastor, our teachers? Why?

Do you have something to tell us? If you do, help us to be ready to listen, ready to hear, ready to share ideas and thoughts, ready to learn, ready to teach with our lives. Amen.

Sarah Klos served as a director of Christian education with the Evangelical Lutheran Church in America for twenty-five years. She is the coauthor of *Sharing God's Mission in the Classroom*, as well as the author of *Prayers: Alone/Together*.

Lord, Broaden Our Ideas

Origen

Let us ask the Lord to broaden our ideas, make them clearer, and bring them nearer to the truth, that we may understand the other things too that he has revealed to his prophets. May we study the Holy Spirit's writings under the guidance of the Spirit himself and compare one spiritual interpretation with another, so that our explanation of the texts may be worthy of God and the Holy Spirit, who inspired them. May we do this through Christ Jesus, our Lord, to whom glory and power belong and will belong through all the ages. Amen.

Born in Alexandria, Egypt, Origen (A.D. 185–254) was raised by Christian parents. His father was killed in the persecution of Alexandria in 202, and Origen was kept from seeking martyrdom by his mother who hid his clothes. He was well known as a preacher and writer, and founded a school at Caesarea in 231. Most of his theological works have disappeared, but his most important is considered to be *De Principiis*. In 250 he was imprisoned and tortured; he survived only a few years after that.

Prayer for Understanding

St. Hilary of Poitiers

Almighty God, bestow upon us the meaning of words, the light of understanding, the nobility of diction and the faith of the true nature. And grant that what we believe we may also speak.

Hilary (ca. 315–67) bishop of Poitiers, was a convert from Neo-platonism and was involved in the Arian disputes for which he was exiled for four years to Phrygia. He is renowned as a defender of orthodoxy and as the most respected Latin theologian laborer of his age. His feast day, January 13, gives his name to the spring term at the Law Courts and at Oxford and Durham Universities in England.

Come to Me in My Mind

Herbert Brokering

Lord, ideas keep coming into my head,
and I don't know where they come from.
They seem to come from deep inside myself,
and they also come from the outside.
In me there lives so much that is new and
    original,
I'm glad for the gift of new thoughts.
Remind me this day of the importance of the
    human mind.
I am responsible;
I am imaginative.
Come to me in my mind, Jesus.

The Reverend Herbert Brokering was a pastor with the Evangelical Lutheran Church in America. He has written a number of books including *The Night Before Jesus*, *Wholly Holy*, *A Pilgrimage to Luther's Germany*, and *In a Promise*. The Reverend Brokering lives in Minneapolis.

The Elixir

George Herbert

Teach me, my God and King,
In all things thee to see,
And what I do in any thing,
To do it as for thee.

Not rudely, as a beast.
To run into an action;
But still to make thee prepossest
And give it his perfection.

A man that looks on glass,
On it may stay his eye;
Or if he pleaseth, through it pass,
And then the heav'n espy.

All may of thee partake:
Nothing can be so mean.
Which with this tincture (for thy sake)
Will not grow bright and clean.

A servant with this clause
Makes drudgery divine:
Who sweeps a room as for thy laws,
Makes that and th' action fine.

This is the famous stone
That turneth all to gold:
For that which God doth touch and own
Cannot for less be told.

English poet George Herbert (1593–1633) became a clergyman
in his thirties and ministered in a small parish near Salisbury.

The Speaking Voice

A. W. Tozer

Lord, teach me to listen. The times are noisy and my ears are weary with the thousand raucous sounds which continuously assault them. Give me the spirit of the boy Samuel when he said to Thee, "Speak, for thy servant heareth." Let me hear Thee speaking in my heart. Let me get used to the sound of Thy Voice, that its tones may be familiar when the sounds of earth die away and the only sound will be the music of Thy speaking Voice. Amen.

Aiden Wilson Tozer (1897–1963) had neither a college nor a seminary education, yet he served for most of his life as a pastor in the Christian and Missionary Alliance, became the editor of *The Alliance Witness*, and authored more than a dozen books. He has been described as an evangelical mystic with a passion for truth. He wrote, "Perception of ideas rather than the storing of them should be the aim of education. The mind should be an eye to see with rather than a bin to store facts in." And, he believed, there is "nothing more wonderful than an alert and eager mind made incandescent by the presence of the indwelling Christ."

Prayer

C. S. Lewis

Master, they say that when I seem
    To be in speech with you,
Since you make no replies, it's all a dream
    —One talker aping two.

They are half right, but not as they
    Imagine; rather I
Seek in myself the things I meant to say,
    And lo! the wells are dry.

Then, seeing me empty, you forsake
    The Listener's role, and through
My dead lips breathe and into utterance wake
    The thoughts I never knew.

Clive Staples Lewis (1898–1963), professor of English literature at the Universities of Oxford and Cambridge, became one of the most popular defenders of Christianity in the twentieth century. He is best known for his apologetic works, *Mere Christianity* and *The Screwtape Letters*, and for his children's fantasies, *The Chronicles of Narnia*.

Live and Learn

John Calvin Reid

I am here reminded, O God, that the school of faith is still in session and that I am a long, long way from graduation.

Forbid that this pupil of yours should be content with the little that I know concerning you and your ways, when there is so much still to learn! "O the depth of the riches both of the wisdom and knowledge of God!"

Every day may I be a humble but earnest seeker after truth—living true to the light I have attained, but never satisfied with it. Rather, may I be among those who follow on to know you, whose ways are ways of pleasantness and whom to know is life and peace. Amen.

John Calvin Reid, author and retired minister, is the former vice-moderator of the United Presbyterian Church in the United States. He pastored a number of Presbyterian churches and was known as a preacher and storyteller. He writes this: "In all churches that I have served, it has been my custom to invite the children to come down to the front of the sanctuary and sit with me on the steps and help me 'tell the story.'"

Take, O Lord, and Receive

Mother Teresa and the Missionaries of Charity

Take, O Lord, and receive
All my liberty, my memory,
my understanding and my will,
all that I have and possess.
You have given them to me;
To you, O Lord, I restore them.
All things are yours:
Dispose of them according to your will.
Give me your love and your grace,
For this is enough for me.

Founder of the Society of the Missionaries of Charity in 1948, Mother Teresa has worked in the slums of Calcutta and in other cities, living out her love of Christ. She writes, "My poor ones in the world's slums are like the suffering Christ. In them God's Son lives and dies, and through them God shows me his true face." She has received the Nobel Peace Prize for her work.

CHAPTER 3

Prayers in Times of Success and Failure

Growth and learning demand risk. Anytime we set about learning—whether we're finally taking the time to tackle that challenging book, embarking on a degree program, reading for our discussion group, composing a paper, or writing a lecture—we expose ourselves to the possibility of failure. Risk is frightening, but necessary, because as Eric Milner-White suggests, we do not have "knowledge enough to need no teaching, wisdom enough to need no correction, talents enough to need no grace." The prayers in this chapter help us as we bolster our courage to face new challenges.

Learning and growth may seem most hazardous for those who have failed, who need to forgive themselves and set the past behind, so that they can get up and begin to grow again. Resolving to put their failure to good use, they need to find what their misfortune says about their fervent interests and get a clearer perspective on their lives. These prayers seek divine resources, so that those who fail may determine not to play it safe.

But risk can also be hard for those who have known success. Our culture encourages expertise; we are often expected to do only what we know we can do easily and well. Often the successful suffer from fear of failure, afraid that what they say might not be profound or that they might lose their high class standing. They need some divine pressure to step out and try some new area of study.

In fact, the difficulty of risk may be common to all of us whether we have (largely) failed or succeeded. It has to do with our sense of who we are. Most of us have heard the imposter syndrome's sinister whisper: "Your understanding, your degree, your enjoyment in learning—they were all a fluke, a mistake! You can't possibly study, learn, and grow."

What we need is a sense of divine perspective, much as Joseph Bernardin prays that "when we do well in work or play, give us a sense of proportion." Failure is inevitable when we risk. When our fear of failure cripples us from taking further risk, or when the learner finds his or her sense of self totally entangled in success, there are danger, unwholeness, and loss of balance.

Left to ourselves, we easily cave in to pressures and lose perspective. We struggle to look honestly at our failures and our successes—we despair or we gloat. In this chapter we bring God our successes and our failures, and we ask for clear vision as we continue to accept challenges, as we resolve to strive for perfection of effort rather than perfection of performance.

Christ,
the Master Carpenter

Iona Community

O Christ, the Master Carpenter
Who, at the last, through wood and nails,
Purchased our whole salvation.
Wield well your tools in the workshop of your
    world,
So that we, who come rough-hewn to your bench,
May here be fashioned to a truer beauty of your
    hand.
We ask it for your own name's sake.

The Iona Community was founded in 1938 by George MacLeod
on the island by the same name off the coast of Scotland. Its
many members also seek to live their common life in the midst
of violence in various urban centers.

Prayer in Time of Failure

W. E. B. Du Bois

O God, teach us to know that failure is as much a part of life as success—and whether it shall be evil or good depends upon the way we meet it—if we face it listlessly and daunted, angrily or vengefully, then indeed is it evil for it spells death. But if we let our failures stand as guideposts and as warnings—as beacons and as guardians—then is honest failure far better than stolen success, and but a part of that great training which God gives us to make us women and men. The race is not to the swift—nor the battle to the strong, O God. Amen.

Educated at Fisk University, Harvard University, and the University of Berlin, W. E. B. Du Bois (1868–1963) was the first African American to receive a doctorate from Harvard. A prolific author of novels, autobiographical sketches, verses, and scholarly studies, including his monumental work, *The Souls of Black Folk*, Du Bois served as professor of economics and sociology at Atlanta University.

Making Possible

Amy Carmichael

May thy grace, O Lord, make that possible to me which seems impossible to me by nature.

Amy Carmichael (1867–1951) served as a Keswick missionary to China for more than half a century. Although she suffered from crippling arthritis after her retirement, she wrote many popular devotional books including *Things as They Are*, *The Beginning of a Story*, and *Lotus Buds*.

A Prayer after Falling

Gregory of Nazianzus

I have deceived myself, dear Christ, I confess it;
I have fallen from the heights to the depths.
O lift me up again, for well I know
delusion came because I wanted it.
If I presume again, I'll fall again,
and fall to my undoing. Take me to you
or I die. It cannot be that I
alone shall find you hard and unresponsive.

Gregory of Nazianzus (329–89) is best known as a theologian
and as one of the "Cappadocian Fathers." After studying at the
University of Athens, he adopted a monastic life. He later
preached eloquently, influencing the church to restore the
Nicene Creed. He was appointed bishop of Constantinople in
381, but resigned to Nazianzus and continued his writing.

For Courage to Hope

Søren Kierkegaard

O Lord, my God, give me again the courage to hope. Merciful God, let hope once again make fertile my sterile and barren mind.

Søren Kierkegaard (1813–55), who lived his whole life at Copenhagen, was the son of a wealthy Lutheran businessman. Always a melancholy man, he is best known for his theological and philosophical writings, which influenced existentialist thinkers as well as theologians like Karl Barth. His more religious books, such as *Christian Discourses* and *Training in Christianity*, show a deep understanding of the Cross.

Acknowledging
Our Need

Eric Milner-White

Suffer me never to think that I have knowledge enough to need no teaching, wisdom enough to need no correction, talents enough to need no grace, goodness enough to need no progress, humility enough to need no repentance, devotion enough to need no quickening, strength sufficient without thy Spirit; lest, standing still, I fall back for evermore.

Eric Milner-White (1884–1964) was dean of York. He founded the Oratory of the Good Shepherd, an Anglican order of priests. He helped to develop the popular service of Nine Lessons and Carols at King's College, Cambridge, and is the author of a number of prayers, hymns, and books including *One God and Father of All* and *My God, My Glory*.

For Light in Times of Darkness

Hildegard of Bingen

The Word made flesh for us gives us the greatest
   hope
that the murky night of darkness will not
   overwhelm us,
but we shall see the daylight of eternity.

Lord, let us receive your clear light;
be for us such a mirror of light
that we may be given grace to see you unendingly.
If we are overcome, you have the power to forgive
   us:
therefore, in my sin I call on you, my Light, for
   help,
for you were sent into the world
to enlighten my heart, to nurture true repentance,
and to make the Holy Spirit's work grow
   powerfully in me.
With the Father and the Holy Spirit
you live and reign for ever!

From the age of three, Hildegard (1098–1179) had visions of
the "living light." She became head of a Benedictine congregation in 1136. Known for her healing and preaching, she
founded several communities and wrote several books.

The Apologist's Evening Prayer

C. S. Lewis

From all my lame defeats and oh! much more
From all the victories that I seemed to score;
From cleverness shot forth on Thy behalf
At which, while angels weep, the audience laugh;
From all my proofs of Thy divinity,
Thou, who wouldst give no sign, deliver me.

Thoughts are but coins. Let me trust, instead
Of Thee, their thin-worn image of Thy head.
From all my thoughts, even from my thoughts of
    Thee,
O thou fair Silence, fall, and set me free.
Lord of the narrow gate and the needle's eye,
Take from me all my trumpery lest I die.

Best known for his apologetic works and his children's fantasies, *The Chronicles of Narnia,* Clive Staples Lewis (1898–1963) was professor of English literature at the Universities of Oxford and Cambridge. He became one of the most popular defenders of Christianity in the twentieth century and also wrote a number of popular works on theological subjects such as suffering and prayer.

Spinning Tops

Kathy Keay

How strange—
we are all so ardent in our piety
so careful not to slip up
so intent on making our individual lives
count in the scheme of things
tyrannized by overfull diaries
driven by the echo of our 'well done.'
And where does it all lead?

Spinning round like tops
we spiral down before You
in now grubby, tattered clothes
out of breath.

Deal gently with us, Lord.

Kathy Keay studied English and education at Oxford and then worked as a freelance writer, editor, and journalist. She has traveled widely, presenting workshops in the United Kingdom, the United States, India, Africa, and South Africa. The author of eight books, she died in late 1994.

For a Sense of Proportion

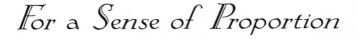

Joseph L. Bernardin

Grant unto us, O Lord, the gift of modesty. When we speak, teach us to give our opinion quietly and sincerely. When we do well in work or play, give us a sense of proportion, that we be neither unduly elated nor foolishly self-deprecatory. Help us in success to realize what we owe to thee and to the efforts of others: in failure, to avoid dejection; and in all ways to be simple and natural, quiet in manner and lowly in thought: through Christ.

Born of Italian immigrant parents, Joseph L. Bernardin grew up in South Carolina and felt a call to the priesthood when he was in college. Now Roman Catholic cardinal of Chicago, he is a recipient of the Albert Einstein International Peace Prize and author of many books.

In All Our Learning Give Us Grace

E. J. Burns

O God, you give to humankind
a searching heart and questing mind;
grant us to find your truth and laws,
and wisdom to perceive their cause.

In all our learning give us grace
to bow ourselves before your face;
as knowledge grows, Lord, keep us free
from self-destructive vanity.

Sometimes we think we understand
all workings of your mighty hand;
then through your Son help us to know
those truths which you alone can show.

Teach us to joy in things revealed,
to search with care all yet concealed;
as through Christ's light your truth we find
and worship you with heart and mind.

Educated at Liverpool and Oxford, E. J. Burns has always lived
in Lancashire. With special interests in biblical studies, the re-
lationship between science and theology, and ethical issues in
medicine, he has pastored a number of churches and served as a
hospital chaplain for twenty years. He has written a number of
hymns.

Lord, in My Success I Need You

Peter Marshall

Lord, forgive me that when life's circumstances lift me to the crest of the wave, I tend to forget Thee. Yet, like an errant child, I have blamed Thee with my every failure, even as I credit myself with every success.

When my fears evaporate like the morning mist, then vainly I imagine that I am sufficient unto myself, that material resources and human resources are enough.

I need Thee when the sun shines, lest I forget the storm and the dark. I need Thee when I am popular, when my friends and those who work beside me approve and compliment me. I need Thee more then, lest my head begin to swell.

O God, forgive me for my stupidity, my blindness in success, my lack of trust in Thee. Be Thou now my Saviour in success. Save me from conceit. Save me from pettiness. Save me from myself! And take this success, I pray, and use it for Thy glory. In Thy strength, I pray. Amen.

Born in 1902, Peter Marshall emigrated from Scotland to the United States, where he trained as a Presbyterian minister and was, in 1947, made chaplain to the United States Senate. He died in 1949.

A Prayer for Contentment

Jeremy Taylor

O Almighty God, Father and Lord of all the creatures, by secret and undiscernible ways bringing
good out of evil: give me wisdom from above;
teach me to be content in all changes of person
and condition, to be temperate in prosperity, and
in adversity to be meek, patient, and resigned; and
to look through the cloud, in the meantime doing
my duty with an unwearied diligence, and an
undisturbed resolution.

Jeremy Taylor (1613–67), an Anglican bishop and writer, was
chaplain to Charles I. After the king's defeat, he escaped to
Wales where he wrote several books including *The Rule and Exercise of Holy Living*, *The Rule and Exercise of Holy Dying*, and
The Golden Grove. He became known for his deep spiritual insight.

Looking Back, Looking Ahead

Aleksandr Solzhenitsyn

How easy it is to live with You, O Lord.
How easy to believe in You.
When my spirit is overwhelmed within me,
When even the keenest see no further than the
    night,
And know not what to do tomorrow,
You bestow on me the certitude
That You exist and are mindful of me,
That all the paths of righteousness are not barred.

As I ascend into the hill of earthly glory,
I turn back and gaze, astonished, on the road
That led me here beyond despair,
Where I too may reflect Your radiance upon
    mankind.

All that I may reflect, You shall accord me,
And appoint others where I shall fail.

Born in 1918, Aleksandr Solzhenitsyn received his training in science. Drafted into the Soviet Red Army in 1941, he was arrested and sent to prison in Siberia in 1945 for criticizing Stalin in a letter to a friend. He became internationally known in 1962 for his novel, *One Day in the Life of Ivan Denisovich*. In 1970, he won the Nobel Prize for literature, but the Soviet government refused to allow him to accept it. Forced into exile four years later, he lived in seclusion in the United States. The collapse of the Soviet Union eventually made it possible for him to return to Russia in 1994.

Go to the Root

Eugene Peterson

I am more comfortable, Father, with an image of you as a gentleman farmer, pruning an occasional branch and raking up a few leaves. But you go to the root. I submit myself to your surgery, and hope in your salvation. Amen.

Eugene Peterson, professor of spiritual theology at Regent College, is the author of numerous books, including *Run with the Horses: A Quest for Life at Its Best* and *Earth and Altar: The Community of Prayer in a Selfbound Society*. He spent many years as pastor of a Presbyterian church in Maryland.

The Task Your Wisdom Has Assigned

Charles Wesley

The task your wisdom has assigned
here let me cheerfully fulfill;
in all my work your presence find
and prove your good and perfect will.

You I would set at my right hand
where eyes my inmost secrets view.
And labor on at your command
and offer all my work to you.

Help me to bear your easy yoke
and every moment watch and pray
and still to things eternal look
and hasten to that glorious day.

Charles Wesley (1707–88) was born the eighteenth child in the family of Susanna and Samuel Wesley. After a missionary trip to Georgia, he returned to England where he wrote more than 5,500 hymns, including "Hark! the Herald Angels Sing," "O For a Thousand Tongues," "Love Divine, All Loves Excelling," and "Christ the Lord Is Risen Today."

CHAPTER 4

Prayers in Times of Stress and Uncertainty

Sometimes learning shakes us up.

Just when we feel secure—we understand the world and our faith pretty well—we take a plunge into learning and find ourselves gasping. We are out of our depth.

At the heart of real learning, miles away from rote memorization or superficial reading, is knowledge which affects us profoundly and touches us deeply. Here we will be changed.

Dazzled with possibilities, dizzied by challenges: we have lost what seemed unshakable. We may find ourselves wishing for "the good old days," only to find that the door has locked behind us.

The prayers in this chapter offer comfort for those who face the challenges and stresses of learning. They remind us that God knows that our quest for knowledge will stretch and extend us. They encourage us to keep pushing at the edges, to be filled with what Louis Untermeyer calls "buoyant doubt" so that we are willing to learn. These prayers remind us that often the only way to peace and wisdom is found by taking the path marked "doubts and darkness," trusting that God is there.

This is what makes the Christian quest for wisdom different. Even when what we learn doesn't make sense or doesn't fit our categories, even when our certainties change—we can rest on the wisdom of the unchangeable God, who is there "Upsetting our easiness / Contradicting our compromises / Replacing our narrow vision." What may appear to us like a step away from faith—a step that we fear will lead to a headlong tumble—is in fact a step of deeper faith. Here we learn to rest in the deep places of God and, as Kierkegaard suggests, "breathe deeply in faith."

Like Peter who abandoned the refuge of the boat to walk toward Jesus, we abandon our securities and find ourselves face to face with ultimate comfort and profound security. We are reminded that Jesus didn't call himself the answer; he called himself the way.

Free Us from the Need to Justify Ourselves

Janet Morley

O God, before whose face
we are not made righteous
even by being right;
free us from the need to justify ourselves
by our own anxious striving,
that we may be abandoned
to faith in you alone,
through Jesus Christ. Amen.

Janet Morley is author of many prayers that were collected in the worship anthology *Celebrating Women*. Adult education advisor for the relief organization Christian Aid, she acted as editor for the collection *Bread of Tomorrow: Praying with the World's Poor*.

When Our Belief Is Perplexed by New Learning

George Ridding

In times of doubts and questionings, when our belief is perplexed by new learning, new teaching, new thought, when our faith is strained by creeds, by doctrines, by mysteries beyond our understanding, give us the faithfulness of learners and the courage of believers in You; give us boldness to examine, and faith to trust all truth; patience and insight to master difficulties; stability to hold fast our traditions with enlightened interpretations, to admit all fresh truth made known to us, and in times of trouble to grasp new knowledge and to combine it loyally and honestly with the old. Amen.

George Ridding (1828–1904) served as headmaster of Winchester College in England and as first bishop of the newly created diocese of Southwell. As an educator, he was known for his reforms and for his expansion of the curriculum. As bishop, he was known for his independent thought, and his advice was frequently sought by his superiors.

When Our Confidence Is Shaken

Fred Pratt Green

When our confidence is shaken
In beliefs we thought secure,
When the spirit in its sickness
Seeks but cannot find a cure,
God is active in the tensions
Of a faith not yet mature.

Solar systems, void of meaning,
Freeze the spirit into stone;
Always our researches lead us
To the ultimate unknown.
Faith must die, or come full circle
To its source in God alone.
In the discipline of praying,
When it's hardest to believe;

In the drudgery of caring,
When it's not enough to grieve;
Faith, maturing, learns acceptance
Of the insight we receive.
God is love, and thus redeems us
In the Christ we crucify;
This is God's eternal answer
To the world's eternal why.
May we in this faith maturing
Be content to live and die!

Fred Pratt Green, a Methodist pastor, started writing plays and poetry when he was in college, publishing three collections of poems. He started writing hymns in his mid-sixties, many of which have been collected in *The Hymns and Ballads of Fred Pratt Green*. (Copyright © 1971 by Hope Publishing Co.)

My Doubting Questions

Eugene Peterson

Instead of suppressing what I am curious about and avoiding the hard questions that get between me and you, O God, teach me how to submit them to your treatment. I want to bring my doubting questions as well as my faithful obedience into your presence. Amen.

Well known for his books, including *Working the Angles: The Shape of Pastoral Integrity* and *The Contemplative Pastor*, Eugene Peterson is professor of spiritual theology at Regent College.

I Need Thee, Lord

Peter Marshall

I do need thee. Lord, I need thee now. I know that I can do without many of the things that once I thought were necessities, but without thee I cannot live, and dare not die.

I needed thee when sorrow came, when shadows were thrown across the threshold of my life, and thou didst not fail me then. I needed thee when sickness laid a clammy hand upon my family, and I cried to thee, and thou didst hear. I needed thee when perplexity brought me to a parting of the ways, and I knew not how to turn. Thou didst indicate the better way. And though the sun is shining around me today, I know that I need thee even in the sunshine, and shall still need thee tomorrow.

I give thee my gratitude for that constant sense of need that keeps me close to thy side. Help me to keep my hand in thine and my ears open to the wisdom of thy voice.

Speak to me, that I may hear thee giving me courage for hard times and strength for difficult places; giving me determination for challenging tasks. I ask of thee no easy way, but just thy grace that is sufficient for every need, so that no matter how hard the way, how challenging the hour, how dark the sky, I may be enabled to overcome.

Born in Scotland, Peter Marshall immigrated to the United States. His life story is told by his wife, Catherine Marshall, in the book, *A Man Called Peter*. Trained as a Presbyterian minister, he was made chaplain to the United States Senate in 1947 and died in 1949.

You Don't Have to Choose Up Sides

Marjorie Holmes

God, it does not help my faith to be with blind and credulous people who have inherited their religion. Or whose beliefs are package-mixed and who accept you only because they have never questioned you, because they do not think.

In many ways they are worse than the skeptics, the agnostics and atheists who doubt you or deny you altogether.

I cannot abide dumb or bigoted people. I want to flee to the intellectuals. I want to be on the side of people who at least have some logical reasons for what they think.

Lord, help me to remember that I don't have to choose up sides. That my own faith has nothing to do with either kind of people.

Faith is my own private need of you reaching out to find you.

Faith is my own intelligence responding to yours.

My faith is my knowledge that in your vast intelligence you created this world—and me.

My faith is my growing conviction that you are not off somewhere running the universe, but here, now, with me. That you care about me.

Thank you for this faith.

Marjorie Holmes is the author of several books and novels including *I've Got to Talk to Somebody*, *God* and *Messiah*.

We Need Your Forgiveness

The St. Hilda Community

We need your forgiveness, merciful God,
For not allowing our complacency to be shattered,
For taking refuge too often in the familiar and the
    certain,
For not believing in the victory of vulnerability,
For not daring to accept your gifts nor claim your
    promises.
Grant us true repentance.
Set us free to hear your word to us.
Set us free to serve you.

.

The St. Hilda Community, which takes its name from Hilda of
Whitby, was founded in 1987 in London.

The Craving for Certainty

Jim Cotter

Spirit of Wisdom,
take from us all fuss,
the clattering of noise,
the temptation to dominate by the power of
    words,
the craving for certainty.
Lead us through the narrow gate of not knowing,
that we may listen and obey,
and come to a place of stillness,
of true conversation and wisdom.

Jim Cotter, author of several books of prayer, including *Prayer in the Morning* and *Prayer at Night*, lives in Sheffield, England, and is well known as a lecturer and retreat leader.

Teach Me to Be Silent

Henri J. M. Nouwen

O Lord Jesus, your words to your Father were born out of your silence. Lead me into this silence, so that my words may be spoken in your name and thus be fruitful. It is so hard to be silent, silent with my mouth, but even more, silent with my heart. There is so much talking going on within me. It seems that I am always involved in inner debates with myself, my friends, my enemies, my supporters, my opponents, my colleagues, and my rivals. But this inner debate reveals how far my heart is from you. If I were simply to rest at your feet and realize that I belong to you and you alone, I would easily stop arguing with all the real and imagined people around me. These arguments show my insecurity, my fear, my apprehensions, and my need for being recognized and receiving attention. You, O Lord, will give me all the attention I need if I would simply stop talking and start listening to you. I know that in the silence of my heart you will speak to me and show me your love. Give me, O Lord, that silence. Let me be patient and grow slowly into this silence in which I can be with you. Amen.

Well known for such books as *Out of Solitude, In the Name of Jesus,* and *The Way of the Desert*, Henri Nouwen is a priest, a professor, and a writer. Born in the Netherlands, he has taught at the University of Notre Dame, Yale Divinity School, and Harvard Divinity School. Most recently he makes his home in L'Arche Community in Canada.

Dear Lord and Father of Mankind

John Greenleaf Whittier

Dear Lord and Father of mankind,
Forgive our foolish ways!
Reclothe us in our rightful mind;
In purer lives Thy service find,
In deeper reverence, praise.

Drop Thy still dews of quietness,
Till all our strivings cease;
Take from our souls the strain and stress,
And let our ordered lives confess
The beauty of Thy peace.

Breathe through the heats of our desire
Thy coolness and Thy balm;
Let sense be dumb, let flesh retire;
Speak through the earthquake, wind and fire,
O still small voice of calm!

John Greenleaf Whittier (1807–92) grew up in a Quaker family on a farm in Massachusetts. He published his first poem at age nineteen, but most of his energies were directed toward the abolition of slavery, writing and editing various antislavery publications. When his masterpiece, "Snow-Bound," appeared in 1866, Whittier achieved national recognition. Many of his poems are no longer read, but a number of his fine hymns endure.

For Faith

Søren Kierkegaard

Teach me, O God, not to torture myself, not to make a martyr out of myself through stifling reflection, but rather teach me to breathe deeply in faith.

Søren Kierkegaard (1813–55), who lived his whole life at Copenhagen, was the son of a wealthy Lutheran businessman. His philosophical works were very influential on thinkers such as Martin Heidegger and Karl Barth. Kierkegaard is considered to be one of the most personal of thinkers; during his lifetime he moved from an aesthetic to a religious and ultimately to a Christian point of view.

Be Present in Our Past, O Lord

Jeannette Lindholm

Lord, you have welcomed us; we come
To pray for healing in your love.
Please, as we wait to meet you here,
All doubts, impediments remove.

Redeem our sorrows; let our tears
Become your healing waters blessed.
And lead us, lost, to quiet streams
Where we shall find ourselves refreshed.

Be present in our past, O Lord,
And in the mem'ry of our days.
When terrors of the night oppress,
Protect us in your strong embrace.

Remind us of your faithfulness,
The promise of your presence, Lord.
And keep us trusting in your grace
Until we greet you whole, restored.

Educated at Concordia College (Moorhead, Minnesota), Indiana University, and the University of Minnesota, Jeannette Lindholm now teaches in the English department at Gordon College in Wenham, Massachusetts. She has written a number of hymns.

I Need Thy Sense of Time

Howard Thurman

I Need Thy Sense of Time
>   Always I have an underlying anxiety about
>   things.
>   Sometimes I am in a hurry to achieve my ends
>   And am completely without patience. It is hard
>   for me to realize
>   That some growth is slow,
>   That all processes are not swift. I cannot always
>   discriminate
>   Between what takes time to develop and what
>   can be rushed,
>   Because my sense of time is dulled.
>   I measure things in terms of happenings.
>   Oh to understand the meaning of perspective
>   That I may do all things with a profound sense
>   of leisure
>   — of time.

I Need Thy Sense of the Future
>   Teach me to know that life is ever
>   On the side of the future.
>   Keep alive in me the forward look, the high
>   hope,
>   The onward surge. Let me not be frozen
>   Either by the past or the present.
>   Grant me, O patient Father, thy sense of the
>   future
>   Without which all life would sicken and die.

Howard Thurman (1900–81) helped to organize the interracial Church for the Fellowship of All Peoples in San Francisco. He wrote more than twenty books on religion and race. His work significantly influenced Martin Luther King, Jr.

Invitation to Ambiguity

Eugene Peterson

I like neat, black-and-white solutions to life, Lord, but the existence you invite me into is ambiguous: there is the miracle of Isaac, but there is also the fact of Ishmael. Like Sarah I would like to banish what doesn't fit into my scheme; but your scheme is larger than mine. Show me how to live in your larger providence. Amen.

After pastoring a church in Maryland for many years, Eugene Peterson has become professor of spiritual theology at Regent College in Vancouver, British Columbia. He is the author of numerous books, including *The Message*.

Searching for Faith

Richard J. Foster

God, today I resonate with the desperate cry in the Gospel, "I believe, help my unbelief." Sometimes I think I operate my life out of more doubt than faith. And yet I want to believe . . . and I do believe.

I'm a complex creature. At times I can believe with my head, while my body is still locked into patterns of skepticism and doubt. Faith is not yet in my muscles, my bones, my glands.

Increase faith within me, O Lord. I'm sure that for faith to grow you will put me in situations where I'll need resources beyond myself. I submit to this process.

Will this mean moving out on behalf of others, praying for them and trusting you to work in them? If so, then show me the who, what, when, and where, and I will seek to act at your bidding. Throughout I am trusting you to take me from faith to faith—from the faith I do have to the faith that I am in the process of receiving.

Thank you for hearing my prayer. Amen.

Well-known writer and teacher, Richard Foster is best known for his writing on the spiritual disciplines including *Celebration of Discipline*, *Freedom of Simplicity*, and *Prayer*. He writes, "Superficiality is the curse of our age. . . . The desperate need today is not for a greater number of intelligent, or gifted people, but for deep people."

Keep Me in the Hollow of Your Hand

Brother Ramon

Lord of the elements and changing seasons, keep me in the hollow of your hand. When I am tossed to and fro with the winds of adversity and the blasts of sickness and misunderstanding, still my racing heart, quiet my troubled mind.

Bring me at last through the storms and tribulations of this mortal life into the calm evening of your unchanging love; and grant that in the midst of my present perplexities and confusion I may experience your peace which passes human understanding.

Brother Ramon is a member of the Anglican Society of St. Francis. He has conducted many spiritual retreats, and he now lives as a hermit.

Prayers of Steel

Carl Sandburg

Lay me on an anvil, O God.
Beat me and hammer me into a crowbar.
Let me pry loose old walls.
Let me lift and loosen old foundations.

Lay me on an anvil, O God.
Beat me and hammer me into a steel spike.
Drive me into the girders that hold a skyscraper
together.
Take red-hot rivets and fasten me into the central
girders.
Let me be the great nail holding a skyscraper
through blue nights into white stars.

Born in Galesburg, Illinois, into a poor, but affectionate family
of Swedish immigrants, Carl Sandburg (1878–1967) found em-
ployment as a migratory laborer, dishwasher, porter, brickmaker,
salesman, and in other jobs. While working as a reporter for a
Chicago newspaper in the early twentieth century, he eventually became very popular as a poet of middle America. His poems often express the voice of a common individual confronted
by the complexities of modern life. Sandburg was also well
known for his *Rootabaga Stories* for children and for a major bi-
ography of Abraham Lincoln.

I Have Not Knowledge

George MacDonald

I have not knowledge, wisdom, insight, thought,
    Nor understanding, fit to justify
Thee in Thy work, O Perfect! Thou hast brought
Me up to this; and lo! what Thou has wrought,
    I cannot comprehend. But I can cry,
    "O enemy, the Maker hath not done;
One day thou shalt behold, and from the sight
    shalt run."

Thou workest perfectly. And if it seem
    Some things are not so well, 'tis but because
        They are too loving deep, too lofty wise,
    For me, poor child, to understand their laws.
My highest wisdom, half is but a dream;
My love runs helpless like a falling stream;
        Thy good embraces ill, and lo! its illness
        dies.

George MacDonald (1824–1905) was born in Scotland and
trained for the ministry in Aberdeen. After losing his first post
on suspicion of heresy, he turned to writing. He wrote a number
of children's books, novels, and more theological works such as
Unspoken Sermons. About MacDonald, C. S. Lewis once said, "I
know hardly any other writer who seems to be closer, or more
continually close, to the Spirit of Christ Himself."

Prayer of a Divided Heart

Countee Cullen

Jesus of the twice-turned cheek,
Lamb of God, although I speak
With my mouth thus, in my heart
Do I play a double part.
Ever at Thy glowing altar
Must my heart grow sick and falter,
Wishing He I served were black,
Thinking then it would not lack
Precedent of pain to guide it,
Let who would or might deride it;
Surely then this flesh would know
Yours had borne a kindred woe.
Lord, I fashion dark gods, too,
Daring even to give You
Dark despairing features where,
Crowned with dark rebellious hair,
Patience wavers just so much as
Mortal grief compels, while touches
Quick and hot, of anger, rise
To smitten cheek and weary eyes.
Lord, forgive me if my need
Sometimes shapes a human creed.

Countee Porter Cullen (1903–46) grew up in Harlem, the
adopted son of a minister to an African Methodist Church. He
graduated Phi Beta Kappa from New York University and received his M.A. from Harvard. His first book of poetry, *Color*,
appeared when he was a college senior.

The Doubter's Prayer

Anne Brontë

Eternal power, of earth and air!
 Unseen, yet seen in all around;
Remote, but swelling everywhere;
 Though silent heard in every sound;

If e'er thine ear in Mercy lent,
 When wretched mortals cried to Thee,
And if indeed, Thy Son was sent,
 To save lost sinners such as me:

Then hear me now, while kneeling here,
 I lift to Thee my heart and eye,
And all my soul ascends in prayer,
 Oh, give me—Give me Faith! I cry.

While Faith is with me, I am blest;
 It turns my darkest night to day;
But while I clasp it to my breast,
 I often feel it slide away.

Anne Brontë (1820–49), like her more famous sisters Emily and
Charlotte, was a successful writer of fiction. The youngest child
in the Brontë family, Anne was educated mainly at the parsonage in Haworth, England. She is best remembered for her novels Agnes Grey and The Tenant of Wildfell Hall.

From One Discovery to Another

Roger Schutz

Although within us there are wounds,
Lord Christ, above all there is
the miracle of your mysterious presence.
Thus, made lighter or even set free,
we are going with you, the Christ,
from one discovery to another.

Roger Schutz sheltered Jews and other refugees in the village of
Taizé, France, during the 1940s. In 1944, he formed an ecu-
menical monastic community, which attracts thousands of pil-
grims each year. Brother Roger is the author of a number of vig-
orous prayers and meditations.

Afraid to Trust You

A. W. Tozer

Father, I want to know Thee, but my coward heart
fears to give up its toys. I cannot part with them
without inward bleeding, and I do not try to hide
from Thee the terror of the parting. I come trem-
bling, but I do come. Please root from my heart all
those things which I have cherished so long, and
which have become a very part of my living self,
so that Thou mayest enter and dwell there without a rival. Then shalt Thou make the place of
Thy feet glorious. Then shall my heart have no
need of the sun to shine in it, for Thyself wilt be
the light of it, and there shall be no night there.

Aiden Wilson Tozer (1897–1963) grew up on a farm in Pennsylvania and was ordained as a minister in the Christian and Missionary Alliance, serving churches in Chicago and Toronto. For
thirteen years he edited *The Alliance Witness* and authored a
number of books, including *The Pursuit of God* and *The Knowledge of the Holy*. A rather quiet man, he was known for his
prayerful life. He once wrote, "When we become too glib in
prayer we are most surely talking to ourselves."

God, Keep Me Still Unsatisfied

Louis Untermeyer

God, though this life is but a wraith,
  Although we know not what we use,
Although we grope with little faith,
  Give me the heart to fight—and lose.

Ever insurgent let me be,
  Make me more daring than devout;
From sleek contentment keep me free,
  And fill me with a buoyant doubt.

Open my eyes to visions girt
  With beauty, and with wonder lit—
But let me always see the dirt,
  And all that spawn and die in it.

Open my eyes to music; let
  Me thrill with Spring's first flutes and drums—
But never let me dare forget
  The bitter ballads of the slums.

From compromise and things half-done,
  Keep me, with stern and stubborn pride.
And when, at last, the fight is won,
  God, keep me still unsatisfied.

Louis Untermeyer (1885–1977) began his career in business, but later became a poet and editor of more than one hundred books and anthologies, including such standard texts as *Modern American Poets* and *Modern British Poetry*. He served as poetry consultant to the Library of Congress, 1961–63.

You Said You Were the Way

Iona Community

Now, when we dream dreams
Or puzzle over the future;
Now, when our ideals are challenged
And the second best becomes attractive,
You are there . . .
Upsetting our easiness,
Contradicting our compromises,
Replacing our narrow vision
With the sight and sound and taste of a better life,
Picking up the loose stitches of our devotion,
Turning the random into the real,
And for this we praise you.

And it always will be so.
For you did not say you were the answer,
You said you were the way;
You did not ask us to succeed,
You asked us to be faithful;
You did not promise us paradise tomorrow,
You said you would be with us to the end of the
   world,
Turning the random into the real.
And for all this we praise you,
now and forever.
Amen.

The Scottish island of Iona is the geographical heart of this community, founded by George MacLeod in 1938. The community also has members in various urban centers where they seek to live their common life in the midst of violence. This excerpt is an appending of a larger prayer written by John L. Bell.

CHAPTER 5

Prayers for Teaching and Discovering

"The school of today is the world of tomorrow," writes W. E. B. Du Bois in the first prayer of this chapter. How we come to view the world, and our place in it, is often most profoundly shaped by our schooling and by those teachers who have worked with us—pointing us in new directions, opening our eyes to a particular discipline, enabling our discovery.

These prayers help us to understand the great work of education as a partnership between those who teach and those who learn, and to see God as collaborating with us in all our learning.

Some of these prayers are intended especially for teachers. "As I prepare for teaching," prays Sarah Klos, "make me first a learner." Gabriela Mistral, humbly aware that Christ was himself a teacher, asks that she "not be pained by the lack of understanding nor saddened by the forgetfulness" of those whom she has taught. And teacher J. M. Cameron asks God's help to induce the "right per-plexities" in his students.

But just as a good teacher does not merely dis-pense knowledge, so, too, God participates with us, collaborating in all of human disciplines. "You take the pen—and the lines dance," praises Dag Hammarskjöld. "You take the flute—and the notes shimmer." Poet e e cummings wonders how any human can "doubt unimaginably You?" while celebrating the senses of tasting, touching, hearing, and seeing. Scholar Jean-Pierre de Caussade sees God speaking through historical events; and Christina Rossetti prays for eyes to see the natural world so that "taught by such, we see / Beyond all creatures thee." In this spirit, then, Walter Rauschenbusch prays that God will grant to teachers "an abiding consciousness that they are coworkers with you, great teacher of humanity."

"School" equips us for the larger "world," not only through the particular discipline we may have mastered, but also through the daily habits and the patterns we acquire in our course of study. A compliment, for example, that changed the day for Marjorie Holmes, leads her to pray that she will "use it more often to heal and lift and fortify others' lives." Mary Stewart prays to be kept from pettiness: "let us be large in thought." Even the very cycle of academic life ("another class, another school year"), which prompts the prayer of Clifford Swartz, can remind us that every new course of study provides us with a fresh start. This, in itself, is a lesson in grace.

While prayers in previous chapters praise the Source of all wisdom, seek God's guidance and direction, or ask for help in facing new challenges, all the prayers in this chapter express in various ways the simple request of Brother Lawrence: "Lord, work with me."

For the Great Work of Education

W. E. B. Du Bois

God bless all schools and forward the great work of education for which we stand. Arouse within us and within our land a deep realization of the seriousness of our problem of training children. On them rests the future work and thought and sentiment and goodness of the world. If here and elsewhere we train the lazy and shallow, the self-indulgent and the frivolous—if we destroy reason and religion and do not rebuild, help us, O God, to realize how heavy is our responsibility and how great the cost. The school of today is the world of tomorrow and today and tomorrow are Thine, O God. Amen.

One of the leading intellectuals of the early twentieth century, W. E. B. Du Bois (1868–1963) served on the board of the NAACP in its formative years. In his influential work, *The Souls of Black Folk*, Du Bois wrote: "The function of the university is not simply to teach bread-winning, or to furnish teachers for the public schools or to be a centre of polite society; it is, above all, to be the organ of that fine adjustment between real life and the growing knowledge of life, an adjustment which forms the secret of civilization."

As I Prepare for Teaching

Sarah Klos

As I prepare for teaching, O God,
Make me first a learner.
Only in this way can I stand in awe
Before your greatness
And, in some small way,
Teach others out of the fullness
Of my own devotion. Amen.

As a director of Christian education for more than twenty-five years, Sarah Klos developed a particular interest in global missions, serving on the board of the Division for World Missions and Ecumenism with the Evangelical Lutheran Church in America.

Grant, O Lord, to All Students

Thomas à Kempis

Grant, O Lord, to all students, to love that which is worth loving, to know that which is worth knowing, to praise that which pleaseth thee most, to esteem that which is most precious unto thee, and to dislike whatsoever is evil in thine eyes. Grant that with true judgment they may distinguish things that differ, and, above all, may search out and do what is well-pleasing unto thee; through Jesus Christ our Lord.

Born near Cologne, Germany, Thomas à Kempis (ca. 1380–1471) entered into a ministry in Holland at about age twenty. There he eventually became the superior while devoting himself to prayer, writing, copying, preaching, teaching, and reading. He lived to be over ninety years old. Originally in Latin, Thomas à Kempis's *Imitation of Christ* is still considered a foremost work of Christian devotion and personal piety.

Lord, Grant Us Eyes to See

Christina Rossetti

Lord, grant us eyes to see
Within the seed a tree,
Within the glowing egg a bird,
Within the shroud a butterfly:
Till taught by such, we see
Beyond all creatures thee,
And hearken for thy tender word
And hear it, "Fear not: it is I."

Christina Rossetti (1830–94), a poet associated with the Pre-
Raphaelite movement in England, was a devout Anglican
whose life was dedicated to the care of her relatives and to
charity. Although troubled by bouts of ill health, she published
several collections of poetry in her lifetime including *Goblin
Market* and *The Prince's Progress*.

You Take the Pen

Dag Hammarskjöld

You take the pen—and the lines dance.
You take the flute—and the notes shimmer.
You take the brush—and the colors sing.
So all things have meaning and beauty in that
    space beyond time where You are.
How, then, can I hold back anything from You?

Dag Hammarskjöld (1905–61) served as the secretary general of
the United Nations from 1953 until 1961. The son of the
Swedish prime minister, he studied law and economics at the
Universities of Uppsala and Stockholm. In his posthumously
published book *Markings* he wrote, "Prayer, crystallized in
words, assigns a permanent wave length on which the dialogue
has to be continued, even when our mind is occupied with
other matters."

The Teacher

Leslie Pinckney Hill

Lord, who am I to teach the way
To little children day by day
So prone myself to go astray?

I teach them knowledge, but I know
How faint they flicker and how low
The candles of my knowledge glow.

I teach them power to will and do,
But only now to learn anew
My own great weakness thru and thru.

I teach them love for all mankind
And all God's creatures, but I find
My love comes lagging far behind.

Lord, if their guide I still must be
Oh, let the little children see
The teacher leaning hard on Thee.

Known as both a teacher and a poet, Leslie Pinckney Hill
(1880–1960) devoted his writing and career to promote high
standards in education as well as emphasizing African American contributions to America. After earning his B.A. and M.A.
from Harvard, Hill contributed poems to collections such as
The Poetry of the Negro and *The Book of American Negro Poems*.
He also published a book of his own poems, *The Wings of Oppression*, and a black verse drama about Haiti called *Toussant
L'Ouverture: A Dramatic History*.

A Prayer for the Teacher

J. M. Cameron

Lord God:
you who are present in all your creatures
and enable them to praise you,
help us to find your image in those we teach
and to ask them useful questions
and induce in them the right perplexities.

J. M. Cameron was born in 1910 in England. After being educated at Oxford, he lectured at a number of universities in the
United Kingdom, Australia, and Canada. He has written several books including *The Arts, Artists and Thinkers*, *Problems in
Psychotherapy and Jurisprudence*, and *John Henry Newman*.

For Those Estranged from You

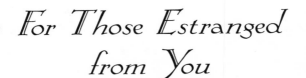

Johann Heermann

O Christ our Light, O radiance true,
Shine forth on those estranged from you,
And bring them to your home again
Where their delight shall never end.

Fill with the radiance of your grace
The wanderer lost in error's maze.
Enlighten those whose secret minds
Some deep delusion haunts and blinds.

Lord, open all reluctant ears
And take away the childish fears
Of those who tremble to express
The faith their secret hearts confess.

Lord, let your mercy's gentle ray
Shine down on others strayed away.
To those in conscience wounded sore,
Show heaven's waiting, open door.

Born near Wohlau in present-day Poland, Johann Heermann (1585–1647) was the fifth and only surviving child whose mother vowed to educate him for the ministry if he survived. He served as pastor in the small town of Köben from 1611–34. Throughout his life, Heermann endured poor health and, later, the ravages of the Thirty Years War. Several times he lost his possessions—and nearly his life—when the town was plundered. Yet out of this adversity, he composed many enduring hymns expressing great depth of feeling and confident faith.

A Teacher's Prayer

Gabriela Mistral

Lord, Thou who didst teach, forgive me for teaching, for bearing the name of teacher which Thou didst bear upon earth. Give me supreme love for my school.

Grant, Master, that my fervor may be enduring and my disappointment transient. Take from me this improper desire for justice which still disturbs me, this base suggestion of protest which rises within me when I am hurt. May I not be pained by the lack of understanding nor saddened by the forgetfulness of those whom I have taught.

A native of Vicuna, Chile, Gabriela Mistral (1889–1957), whose real name is Lucila Godoy de Alcayaga, took her pen name from two poets she admired. She did her elementary education at home and began teaching in a rural school at fifteen. Mistral dedicated herself to education and diplomacy from 1924, working with the Pan-American Union, the League of Nations, and the United Nations, and teaching at Barnard, Vassar, and Middlebury. She continued writing all this time and received the 1945 Nobel Prize for literature.

A Prayer for Teachers

Walter Rauschenbusch

We implore thy blessing, O God, on all the men and women who teach the children and youth of our nation, for they are the potent friends and helpers of our homes. Into their hands we daily commit the dearest that we have, and as they make our children, so shall future years see them. Grant them an abiding consciousness that they are coworkers with you, great teacher of humanity, and that you have charged them with the holy duty of bringing forth from the budding life of the young the mysterious stores of character and ability which you have hidden in them.

A Baptist minister, theologian, and educator, Walter Rauschenbusch (1861–1918) urged Christians to ally themselves with the working class and to seek social reform. His major work, *A Theology for the Social Gospel,* helped to shape the social gospel movement of the early twentieth century.

In Time of Examination

Katharine Lee

O God, who didst give Thy Holy Spirit to guide and strengthen Thy people, fill us now with this same spirit that we may approach the coming examinations with a quiet mind. May the flame of Thy Spirit illumine our thinking and strengthen us to rise above any temptation that may beset us. Grant us a good memory and a wise understanding of what we have learned. May all that we undertake be done to the best of the ability which Thou gavest us. This we ask in the name of Thy dear Son, who Himself was a teacher, Jesus Christ, Our Lord.

Katharine Lee was principal of the National Cathedral School for girls from 1950–68. Born to outstanding parents—her father was a general in the United States Army and her mother helped to organize the nurses's branch of the army after the Spanish-American War—Lee herself received her B.A. from Mount Holyoke and her M.A. from Columbia University. After teaching at several schools in the United States and England, she came to the Cathedral School, where she was especially well known for her chapel talks and Bible classes.

Another School Year

Clifford Swartz

Another class, another school year, Lord.
Tomorrow I must set the tone
For attention to mechanical
Procedures such as grading curves.
They'll listen carefully to that!
These crass details are part of teaching.
As with any trade, we must establish
Rules and then know how to break them.

Bur first, I think I'll ask these students
Where we are. It's easy to forget.
At times the world seems little larger
Than our campus, and for the young
It sometimes shrinks until there's barely
Room enough for one—or if they're lucky, two.
The world is wide in many ways.
In every course we should take journeys
To the boundaries of our knowledge.
The teacher's role in this is not
To specify and plot old routes.
These, the students find embedded
In their texts, complete with diagrams.

Instead, we serve as guides, who have gone down
These roads before, but have not taken
All the side paths, and have not reached the end.
We must be sure our students know
That there are roads we have not taken.
We must prepare them to abandon us

Besides writing prayers, Clifford Swartz has written two books
on physics, *A Search for Order in the Physical Universe* and *Prelude to Physics*. He is the editor of *The Physics Teacher*.

And forge ahead when we turn back.
All we can do is choose the early paths
And with delight cry out, "Oh, look!"
At sights along the way.

Another year, another journey, Lord.
I hope that on a distribution curve
Of distance gone and paths explored
My students all may earn high grades.
But failing that, I pray that I can use such skill
In crying "Look, oh, look!" that each, if only
    once,
May answer with excitement, "Yes, I see, I see!"

Stargazing

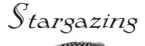

John Calvin Reid

To the gift of sight with which you have endowed me, O God, I pray that you will add the gift of insight. When I gaze upon your handiwork in the sky, may I read its meaning for my soul.

As the planets revolve around the sun obedient to your law, may I make you the center around which I live and move and have my being.

By lifting my eyes to the glory that is above me, may I be led to think lofty thoughts and to seek the things that are above, that heaven may be no strange place to my soul when in due time I take my journey there. Amen.

Born in South Carolina and educated in Pittsburgh, Edinburgh, and Oxford, John Calvin Reid pastored a number of Presbyterian churches. He has written several books including *Parables from Nature*, *Secrets from Field and Forest*, and *Thirty Favorite Bible Stories*.

Teach Me, Lord, to Read the Book of Life

Jean-Pierre de Caussade

You speak, Lord, to all men in general through general events. Revolutions are simply the tides of your Providence, which stir up storms and tempests in people's minds. You speak to men in particular through particular events, as they occur moment by moment. But instead of hearing your voice, instead of respecting events as signals of your loving guidance, people see nothing else but blind chance and human decision. They find objections to everything you say. They wish to add to or subtract from your Word. They wish to change and reform it.

Teach me, dear Lord, to read clearly this book of life. I wish to be like a simple child, accepting your word regardless of whether I understand your purposes. It is enough for me that you speak.

As a Jesuit priest in France, Jean-Pierre de Caussade (1675–1751) taught that God is present in all events, and that we should submit to his will. Two centuries after his death, his talks were published under the title *Self-Abandonment to Divine Providence*.

I Thank You God

e e cummings

i thank You God for most this amazing
day:for the leaping greenly spirits of trees
and a blue true dream of sky; and for everything
which is natural which is infinite which is yes

(i who have died am alive again today,
and this is the sun's birthday;this is the birth
day of life and of love and wings:and of the gay
great happening illimitably earth)

how should tasting touching hearing seeing
breathing any—lifted from the no
of all nothing—human merely being
doubt unimaginably You?

(now the ears of my ears awake and
now the eyes of my eyes are opened)

When Edward Estlin Cummings (1894–1962) was born in
Cambridge, Massachusetts, his father was teaching in the English department at Harvard. Later his father became the pastor
of the famous Old South Church in Boston. Edward Estlin received his B.A. and M.A. from Harvard, and then served in an
ambulance corps in World War I. His poems continue to delight readers with their experiments in punctuation, phrasing,
and stream-of-consciousness techniques.

For Those Who Create or Report

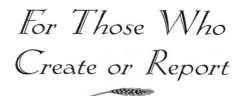

Walter Rauschenbusch

We praise you for our brothers and sisters, the masters of form and color and sound, who have power to unlock for us the vaster spaces of emotion and to lead us by their hand into the reaches of nobler passions. We rejoice in their gifts and pray you to save them from the temptations which beset their powers. Save them from the discouragements of a selfish ambition and from the vanity that feeds on cheap applause, from the snare of the senses and from the dark phantoms that haunt the listening soul.

O thou great source of truth and knowledge, we remember before thee all whose calling it is to gather and winnow the facts for informing the people. Inspire them with a determined love for honest work and a stanch hatred for the making of lies, lest the judgments of our nation be perverted and we be taught to call light darkness and darkness light. Since the sanity and wisdom of a nation are in their charge, may they count it shame to set the baser passions of men on fire for the sake of gain. May they never suffer themselves to be used in drugging the mind of the people with falsehood and prejudice.

Walter Rauschenbusch (1861–1918) was a Baptist minister, theologian, and educator. He dedicated himself to social reform and wrote several books including *Christianity and the Social Crisis*.

Prayer of Learned Yearning

Katherine Juul Nevins

The night before the last day of class—
A strange time to be reflecting on
wishes and hopes and dreams and prayers
for those who have spent every weekday morning
listening to names and dates,
remembering something, or maybe nothing
of consequence.
        Yet, it is the stories that I want them to hear.
Others' stories that come alive,
so that they might become more intrigued with
    their own.

I wish for them

To draw wisdom from lessons in failure,
in lives worn down, worn thin, worn out;
and lessons of triumph from those who persevered,
    overcame,
adapted, adopted, transpired,
    transformed . . . changed.

I wish for them

To be thankful for the women who bore them,
for their matriarchal lineage that endured great
    pain

Katherine Juul Nevins grew up in Kansas. She is professor of
psychology at Bethel College (Minnesota) and focuses on
women's concerns and development, conflict resolution, and or-
ganizational facilitation. She loves music, woodworking, and
nature.

to further the gift of life.
To be thankful for the women who go before
    them:
ordinary women doing extraordinary things,
now extraordinary women doing ordinary things,
who carved a path for themselves in treacherous
    terrains
that we might later come to stroll more freely
    among the hills and plains.

To be thankful for who they are and will become:
more centered, more holy,
never sure, but more secure
in the discovery of themselves,
the giving of gifts, the fulfillment of their calling.

God, nurture the inner light that they might shine
    in any darkness,
And let no human hinder their way.
May they know Joy.
May they know Love.
May they know Peace.
Amen.

The Compliment

Marjorie Holmes

I want to suggest a new Beatitude: "Blessed are the sincere who pay compliments."

For I have just had a compliment, and it has changed my day.

I was irritated. Tired. Discouraged. Nothing seemed much use. Now suddenly all this is changed.

I feel a spurt of enthusiasm, of energy and joy. I am filled with hope. I like the whole world better, and myself, and even you.

Lord, bless the person who did this for me.

He probably hasn't the faintest idea how his few words affected me. But wherever he is, whatever he's doing, bless him. Let him too feel this sense of fulfillment, this recharge of fire and faith and joy.

Thank you, God, for this simple miracle so available to all of us. And that we don't have to be saints to employ its power.

Remind me to use it more often to heal and lift and fortify others' lives: a compliment!

Author and columnist Marjorie Holmes taught adult education writing courses at several universities, and has long been associated with the Georgetown University Writers Conference. She is the author of many novels and articles in popular magazines.

Keep Us, Oh God, From Pettiness

Mary Stewart

Keep us, Oh God, from pettiness; let us be large in
thought, in word, in deed.
Let us be done with fault-finding and leave off
self-seeking.
May we put away all pretense and meet each other
face to face—without self-pity and without
prejudice.
May we never be hasty in judgment and always
generous.
Let us take time for all things; make us to grow
calm, serene, gentle.
Teach us to put into action our better impulses,
straightforward and unafraid.
Grant that we may realize that it is the little
things that create differences, that in the big
things of life we are at one.
And may we strive to touch and to know the
great, common heart of us all, and, Oh Lord
God, let us forget not to be kind!

A scholar of classical literature, Mary Stewart (1878–1943)
served as superintendent of education for the Indians of California. She campaigned vigorously for the causes of women.

Lord, Work with Me

Brother Lawrence

My God, since You are with me, and since it is Your will that I should apply my mind to these outward things, I pray that You will give me the grace to remain with You and keep company with You.

But so that my work may be better, Lord, work with me; receive my work and possess all my affections. Amen.

Born in France, Brother Lawrence (1611–91) had no formal education and served as a soldier and servant. In 1666 he became a lay brother in the Carmelite Order in Paris where he worked in the kitchen until eighty years of age. His life modeled a blending of work and prayer. This prayer is from his famous book, *The Practice of the Presence of God*.

CHAPTER 6

Prayers for Vision Beyond

Deeper wisdom and understanding: with their joys come responsibilities and stresses. Complacency and superiority lure us; we are tempted to settle down, put our feet up, and ponder all we have learned. Sometimes we wish that the privilege of learning didn't have fine print at the bottom, calling us to look in new directions.

Wisdom calls us: she compels us to look within. People we think of as wise have the quality of seeing themselves clearly. They don't fly off in any number of directions, but they wait for the vision to act. And perhaps most important, they act out of a clear sense of being loved—a sense, as Kierkegaard prays, that God has "loved us first."

But the gaze inside becomes a look outside as we turn to look deeply at the world. Wisdom compels us to try to see the world from God's perspective. We look beyond ourselves for a vision of a "world as love would make it." Deeper understanding brings us deeper compassion; we ask with Walter Rauschenbusch, "though increase of knowledge bring increase of sorrow, may we . . . offer ourselves as instruments of your spirit in bringing order and beauty out of disorder and darkness." This vision can be painful.

And the vision can be challenging. The prayers in this chapter are requests not only for understanding and vision, but also for the wisdom to use our newfound knowledge. Finding ways to move forward may be the most demanding work we ever do. We pray for the courage to create, following in the path of our creator God; we pray for the will to work.

These are prayers of courage rather than comfort, of challenge rather than solace. Our learning, soaked with much prayer, leads to wisdom and our wisdom to vision, "till our goals and [God's] are one." This is the life of risking faith that Augustine prays about, in which we find ourselves walking with the God "whom to serve is perfect freedom."

The Knowledge of God

Augustine

Eternal God, who are the light of the minds that know thee, the joy of the hearts that love thee, and the strength of the wills that serve thee: Grant us so to know thee that we may truly love thee, and so to love thee that we may fully serve thee, whom to serve is perfect freedom, in Jesus Christ our Lord.

Augustine (354–430) is generally regarded as the father of the Western church. Born to a devout Christian mother in what is now Algeria, he was raised in the Christian faith, but in his youth, he rebelled against it, both socially and intellectually. He became a skilled rhetorician, and he eventually experienced a wonderful conversion while reading Romans 13 in a garden. By 396, he had become a Catholic bishop, and through his writings vigorously defended the church against attacks from the Manicheists, the Donatists, and the Pelagians. Living and writing during the collapse of the Roman Empire, he developed the doctrines of original sin, predestination, and grace, which were to shape the teachings of the medieval church.

Help Us to Do Our Daily Work

John R. W. Stott

O Lord, Jesus Christ, who at the carpenter's bench didst manifest the dignity of honest labor, and dost give to each of us our tasks to perform: Help us to do our daily work with readiness of mind and singleness of heart, not with eye-service as men-pleasers, but as thy servants, labouring heartily as unto thee and not unto men, so that whatever we do, great or small, may be to the glory of thy holy name.

Educated at Cambridge, John R. W. Stott was ordained in the Anglican Church in 1945 and is best known as a leader in the Anglican evangelical movement. He is well known as a teacher in the Anglican Church worldwide, as well as author of many books ranging from theological commentaries on the New Testament, such as *The Message of Galatians* and *The Message of Thessalonians*, to an evangelistic book such as *Basic Christianity* to a major study called *The Cross of Christ*. Stott directs the London Institute for Contemporary Christianity and is an avid bird watcher.

For Integrity

Robert A. Raines

O God, make me discontent with things the way
   they are in the world,
   and in my own life.
Teach me how to blush again,
   for the tawdry deals,
      the arrogant-but-courteous prejudice,
      the snickers,
      the leers,
      the good food and drink which make me
        too weary to repent,
      the flattery given and received,
      my willing use of rights and privileges
        other men are unfairly denied.
Make me notice the stains when people get spilled
   on.
Make me care about the slum child downtown,
      the misfit at work,
      the people crammed into the
        mental hospital,
      the men, women, and youth
        behind bars.
Jar my complacence; expose my excuses; get me
   involved
   in the life of my city,
   and give me integrity once more.

Robert A. Raines was born in Massachusetts and educated at
Yale and Cambridge before being ordained as a Methodist minister in 1953. He has pastored a number of churches and has
run a retreat and study center. He has written a number of
books including *Reshaping the Christian Life*, *Creative Brooding*,
The Secular Congregation, and *Going Home*.

Spirit of Integrity

Janet Morley

Spirit of integrity,
you drive us into the desert
to search out our truth.
Give us clarity to know what is right,
and courage to reject what is strategic;
that we may abandon the false innocence
of failing to choose at all,
but may follow the purposes of Jesus Christ.
Amen.

Activist, writer, and editor, Janet Morley works as adult education advisor for Christian Aid, a relief organization. Her collections include *Celebrating Women* and *Bread of Tomorrow: Praying with the World's Poor*.

Prayer for Vision

W. E. B. Du Bois

Grant us, O God, the vision and the will to be found on the right side in the great battle for bread, which rages round us, in strike and turmoil and litigation. Let us remember that here as so often elsewhere no impossible wisdom is asked of men, only Thine ancient sacrifice—to do justly and love mercy and walk humbly—to refuse to use, of the world's goods, more than we earn, to be generous with those that earn but little and to avoid the vulgarity that flaunts wealth and clothes and ribbons in the face of poverty. These things are the sins that lie beneath our labor wars, and from such sins defend us, O Lord. Amen.

As an undergraduate at Fisk University, W. E. B. Du Bois (1868–1963) spent his summers teaching at rural schools in Tennessee and was deeply moved by the effects of chronic racial oppression he witnessed. Years later, as a professor of economics and sociology at Atlanta University (1897–1910), he wrote this prayer, among many others, for his students.

A Truer Knowledge
of God

Caryll Houselander

Grant to us, Lord,
that the shock of the first sin,
of the first failure
at the beginning of life,
may give us self-knowledge
and a truer knowledge of You;
may help us to know ourselves
and You,
and to know the depths of Your love.
May it teach us
our dependence on You,
and that without You
we can do nothing.

Turn the humiliation
caused by our vanity
into Your humility,
and lift us up in Your power
and with Your courage
to take the cross
and to start again on the way,
trusting now,
not in ourselves
but in You.

Associated with an advertising firm in London, Caryll House-
lander (1901–54) also sculpted, wrote, and illustrated books.
Her works include *The Way of the Cross*, *The Comforting of
Christ*, *The Reed of God*, and *A Rocking Horse Catholic*. Her con-
temporary and collaborator, Maisie Ward, described her as "that
Divine Eccentric."

Prayer for a World Vision

Peter Marshall

Our Father, with so much bitterness abroad in the
world—this poor bleeding world, stumbling from
blunder to blunder, hollow with graves, hard with
hate—may we who own the name of Christ, shed
abroad Thy love.

We pray for a broader vision of the needs of all
mankind, and a deeper compassion to fill those
needs; for a planting of the seeds of concern for all
humanity in our hearts; for a tapping of the wells
of generosity.

> Help us to live together as people who have
> been forgiven a great debt.
> Help us to be gentle, walking softly with one another.
> Help us to be understanding, lest we shall add
> to the world's sorrow or cause to flow one
> needless tear.
> Help us to stand for what is right, not because it
> may yield dividends later, but because it is
> right now.
> Help us to be as anxious that the rights of
> others shall be recognized as we are that our
> own shall be established.
> Help us to be as eager to forgive others as we are
> to seek forgiveness.
> Help us to know no barriers of creed or race,
> that our love may be like Thine—a love that
> sees all men as Thy children and our brothers.

God, help us all to be ministers of mercy and am-
bassadors of kindness for Jesus' sake. Amen.

Scottish-born Peter Marshall was a Presbyterian minister and
chaplain to the U.S. Senate from 1947 to his death in 1949. He
is author of *Mr. Jones, Meet the Master, Prayers Offered by the
Chaplain*, and *Peter Marshall Speaks*.

Be Thou My Vision

Traditional Gaelic Hymn

Be thou my vision, O Lord of my heart;
Naught be all else to me, save that thou art.
Thou my best thought, by day or night,
Waking or sleeping, thy presence my light.

Be thou my wisdom, and thou my true word;
I ever with thee and thou with me, Lord;
Thou and thou only, first in my heart,
Great God of heaven, my treasure thou art.

Great God of heaven, my victory won,
May I reach heaven's joys, O bright heaven's Sun!
Heart of my own heart, whatever befall,
Still be my vision, O Ruler of all.

This beloved hymn is of Irish origin from around 700. It was
translated by Eleanor H. Hull (1860–1935), versified by Mary
Elizabeth Byrne (1880–1931).

Come to Us, Creative Spirit

Francis Pott

Come to us, creative Spirit.
In our Father's house;
every human talent hallow,
hidden skills arouse,
that within your earthly temple,
wise and simple
may rejoice.

Poet, painter, music-maker
all your treasures bring,
craftsman, actor, graceful dancer
make your offering,
join your hands in celebration;
let creation
shout and sing!

Word from God eternal springing
fill our minds, we pray;
and in all artistic vision
give integrity:
may the flame within us burning
kindle yearning
day by day.

Born in London and educated at Oxford, Francis Pott
(1832–1909) was pastor of a number of churches until his increasing deafness forced him to retire. He then devoted himself
to translating Latin and Syriac hymns and writing many original hymns. He is best remembered for the hymns "Angel Voices
Ever Singing" and "The Strife Is O'er, the Battle Done."

Give Us, O God, a Vision of Your World

Women's World Day of Prayer

Give us, O God, a vision of your world as love
   would make it;
a world where the weak are protected and none go
   hungry;
a world whose benefits are shared, so that
   everyone can enjoy them;
a world whose different people and cultures live
   with tolerance and mutual respect;
a world where peace is built with justice,
and justice is fired with love;
Lord Jesus Christ, give us the courage to build.

This anonymous prayer was used for the 1993 Women's World
Day of Prayer. It is included in Kathy Keay's collection, *Laughter, Silence and Shouting: An Anthology of Women's Prayers*.

God, Who Stretched the Spangled Heavens

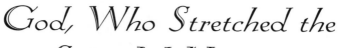

Catherine Cameron

God, who stretched the spangled heavens,
Infinite in time and place,
Flung the suns in burning radiance
Through the silent fields of space,
We your children, in your likeness,
Share inventive powers with you.
Great Creator, still creating,
Show us what we yet may do.

Proudly rise our modern cities,
Stately buildings, row on row;
Yet their windows, blank, unfeeling,
Stare on canyoned streets below,
Where the lonely drift unnoticed
In the city's ebb and flow,
Lost to purpose and to meaning,
Scarcely caring where they go.

As each far horizon beckons
May it challenge us anew.
Children of creative purpose,
Serving others, honoring you.
May our dreams prove rich with promise,
Each endeavor well begun.
Great Creator, give us guidance
Till our goals and yours are one.

Born in New Brunswick, Canada, Catherine Cameron studied English literature at MacMaster's University. She received her graduate degrees from the University of Southern California. Dr. Cameron is Professor Emeritus of Sociology at the University of La Verne. (Copyright © 1967 by Hope Publishing Co.)

A Prayer for Those without Knowledge

Walter Rauschenbusch

We pray for those who amid all the knowledge of our day are still without knowledge; for those who hear not the sighs of the children that toil, nor the sobs of such as are wounded because others have made haste to be rich; for those who have never felt the hot tears of the mothers of the poor that struggle vainly against poverty and vice. Arouse them, we beseech you, from their selfish comfort and grant them the grace of social repentance. Smite us all with the conviction that for us ignorance is sin, and that we are indeed our brother's keeper if our own hand has helped to lay him low. Though increase of knowledge bring increase of sorrow, may we turn without flinching to the light and offer ourselves as instruments of your spirit in bringing order and beauty out of disorder and darkness.

A Baptist minister, theologian, and educator, Walter Rauschenbusch (1861–1918) urged Christians to ally themselves with the working class and to seek social reform. His books, including *Christianizing the Social Order* and *A Theology for the Social Gospel*, were formative to many Christians early this century.

Send Us Out

Sheila Cassidy

Lord of the Universe
look in love upon your people.
Pour the healing oil of your compassion
on a world that is wounded and dying.
Send us out in search of the lost,
to comfort the afflicted,
to bind up the broken,
And to free those trapped
under the rubble of their fallen dreams.

Born in Australia, Sheila Cassidy went to medical school in
England. In 1975, when she was practicing medicine in Chile,
she was arrested and tortured for treating a revolutionary. She is
now medical director of St. Luke's Hospice in Plymouth, England.

Teach Me the Dignity of Labor

F. B. Meyer

Almighty God, teach me the dignity of labor, the honor of industrious toil, the glory of being able to do something in the world. Forgive, I pray thee, my shortcomings and failure, prosper and establish the work of my hands. Make my life deeper, stronger, richer, gentler, more Christlike, more full of the spirit of Heaven, more devoted to thy service and glory. Amen.

Born in London and ordained as a Baptist minister, F. B. Meyer (1847–1929) was a Bible expositor and the author of some forty books. He preached widely throughout the world.

For Renewal

George Appleton

O my God,
grant that I may so wait upon thee,
that when quick decision and action are needed
I may mount up with wings as an eagle;
and when under direction of thy will
and the needs of people
I have to keep going under pressure,
I may run and not be weary;
and in times of routine and humble duty,
I may walk and not faint.
For all my fresh springs are in thee,
O God of my strength.

Born in 1902, George Appleton became an Anglican priest and
served in England, Burma, India, and Australia. In 1968 he was
appointed Anglican archbishop in Jerusalem, where he sought
to build bridges between the Christian, Jewish, and Muslim
communities.

Govern All by Thy Wisdom

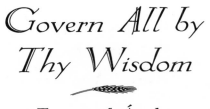

Teresa of Ávila

Govern all by thy wisdom, O Lord, so that my soul may be serving thee as thou dost will, and not as I may choose. Do not punish me, I beseech thee, by granting that which I wish or ask, if it offend thy love, which would always live in me. Let me die to myself, that I may serve thee, who in thyself art the true life. Amen.

Descended from an old Spanish family, Teresa of Ávila (1515–82) entered a Carmelite monastery at age twenty. Throughout her life she established houses of prayer and wrote of her deepening spiritual experiences and instructions for the life of prayer.

Burdens

John Calvin Reid

I would remember, O God, that there are some burdens I am called upon to carry—the burden of responsibility, the burden of honest labor, the burden of duty, the burden of sympathetic concern for the needs of others. I pray not for relief from these burdens, but for strength to bear them with courage and cheerfulness.

But I would remember also that I am not called to carry the burden of guilt, of fear, of anxiety. I pray for relief from these, that my shoulders may be free and strong to carry the burdens I should bear.

Above all, so fill my heart with the spirit of Christ that I shall find his yoke easy and his burden light. Amen.

John Calvin Reid pastored a number of Presbyterian churches during his ministry. He also wrote many books including several children's books, because of, as he writes, "my strong conviction that there should be something special for [children] in every church service, as well as for adults."

Still Let Thy Wisdom Be My Guide

John Wesley

Still let thy wisdom be my guide,
Nor take thy flight from me away;
Still with me let thy grace abide,
That I from thee may never stray:
Let thy word richly in me dwell,
Thy peace and love my portion be;
My joy to endure and do thy will,
Till perfect I am found in thee. Amen.

Fifteenth child of Samuel and Susanna Wesley, John Wesley (1703–91) was educated at Oxford and traveled with his brother Charles on a ministry trip to Georgia. He had a conversion experience in 1738, and he became a well-known preacher and the leader of the Methodist movement.

You Who Have Loved Us First

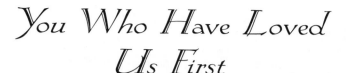

Søren Kierkegaard

You who have loved us first, O God—alas, we speak about it as if it were something historical, that you have loved us first only that one time, and yet you do it constantly; many times every single day throughout life you always love us first. When we awake in the morning and turn our thoughts to you—you are the first, you have loved us first. Even if I arise at daybreak and instantly turn my thoughts to you in prayer, you are too quick for me; you have loved me first. When I collect my thoughts from all my distractions and meditate on you, you are the first. And so it is always—and then we talk ungratefully as if it were but once that you loved us first.

Although better known for his philosophical writings, which had a powerful influence on the existential movement, the devotional writings of Søren Kierkegaard (1813–55), such as *Christian Discourses* and *Training in Christianity*, show a deep and personal Christian faith.

To Work, and Speak, and Think for Thee

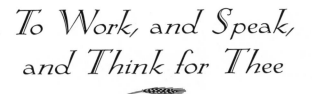

Charles Wesley

Jesu, confirm my heart's desire
    To work, and speak, and think for thee;
Still let me guard the holy fire,
    And still stir up thy gift in me;

Ready for all thy perfect will,
    My acts of faith and love repeat,
Till death thy endless mercies seal
    And make the sacrifice complete.

Charles Wesley (1707–88) was the eighteenth child of Samuel and Susanna Wesley, and a well-known preacher and hymn writer. Author of more than 5,500 hymns, Charles understood their importance for devotional purposes. Some of his most famous hymns include "Lo, He Comes with Clouds Descending" and "Hail the Day that Sees Him Rise."

Make Me Willing to Be Used by You

Alan Paton

Lord, make me willing to be used by you. May my knowledge of my unworthiness never make me resist being used by you. May the need of others always be remembered by me, so that I may ever be willing to be used by you.

And open my eyes and my heart that I may this coming day be able to do some work of peace for you.

Political and social activist, educator and writer, Alan Paton (1903–88) was born in Natal, South Africa. He taught school and was principal of a reformatory for a number of years. He is best known for his novels *Cry the Beloved Country* (1948) and *Too Late the Phalarope* (1953). Paton also wrote a number of nonfiction works on suffering and South Africa.

Benediction

Teresa of Ávila

Christ has no body now on earth but yours;
yours are the only hands with which he can do his
    work,
yours are the only feet with which he can go about
    the world,
yours are the only eyes through which his
    compassion
can shine forth upon a troubled world.
Christ has no body on earth now but yours.

Teresa of Ávila (1515–82) is best known as a person who combined a deep spiritual prayer life with ceaseless activity as an organizer and reformer, showing that the life of prayer can be a dynamic force for action in the world.

Permissions and Acknowledgments

Grateful acknowledgment is made to the following for permission to reprint previously published material.

Chapter 1

Creed ("In You I Believe") from the Nicaraguan Mass "Misa Campesina" in J. M. Vigil and A. Torrellas, *Misas Centro Americanas* (CAV-CEBES 1988). Reprinted in *Bread of Tomorrow* ed. by Janet Morley. Copyright © Christian Aid, London, 1992. Reprinted by permission of Carlos Mejias Godoy.

Elliot, Elisabeth. "Teach Me to Know You Here on Earth." Reprinted by permission of Elisabeth Elliot.

Selected prayer from page 66 from *Prayers from the Heart* by Richard J. Foster. Copyright © 1994 by Richard J. Foster. Reprinted by permission of HarperCollins Publishers, Inc.

Excerpt "Great God of All Wisdom, of Science and Art" by Jane Parker Huber reproduced from *A Singing Faith*. Copyright © 1987 by Jane Parker Huber. Used by permission of Westminster John Knox Press.

Excerpt from *With Christ in the School of Prayer* by Andrew Murray. Copyright © 1981. Reprinted by permission of Whitaker House, 580 Pittsburgh Street, Springdale, PA 15144.

Excerpt "All-Wise God" from *Praying with Moses* by Eugene H. Peterson. Copyright © 1994 by Eugene H. Peterson. Reprinted by permission of HarperCollins Publishers, Inc.

Excerpt from *Prayers from the Nave* by Clifford Swartz. Copyright © 1981 by Clifford E. Swartz. Published by Flax Pond Press. Reprinted by permission.

Excerpt "Praise the Source of Faith and Learning," from *Borrowed Light* by Thomas Troeger. Copyright and reproduced by permission of Oxford University Press, Inc.

Chapter 2

Excerpt "Come to Me in My Mind," from *Surprise Me, Jesus* by Herbert Brokering. Copyright © 1973 Augsburg Publishing House. Reprinted by permission of Augsburg Fortress.

Excerpt from *If You Will Ask* by Oswald Chambers. Copyright © 1958 by Oswald Chambers Publications Assoc. Ltd. U.S. Copyright © 1985 by Chosen Books. Used by permission of Discovery House Publishers, Box 3566, Grand Rapids MI 49501. All rights reserved.

146

Chapter 3

Excerpt by Joseph Bernardin from *The Journalist's Prayer Book* edited by Alfred Klauser and John DeMott. Copyright © 1987 Augsburg Publishing House. Reprinted by permission of Augsburg Fortress.

Excerpt by E. J. Burns from *Hymns for Today's Church*, published by Hodder and Stoughton. Reprinted by permission of E. J. Burns.

Excerpt from *Candles in the Dark* by Amy Carmichael. Copyright © 1981 The Dohnavur Fellowship. Used by permission of The Christian Literature Crusade, Fort Washington, PA, publisher.

Excerpt reprinted *Prayers for Dark People,* by W. E. B. Du Bois, ed. by Herbert Aptheker (Amherst: University of Massachusetts Press, 1980) copyright © 1980 by The University of Massachussetts Press.

Anonymous, from *The Iona Community Worship Book* (Wild Goose Publications, 1991). English text copyright © Iona Community, Glasgow G51 3UU, Scotland, UK.

Excerpt "Spinning Tops" by Kathy Keay from *Laughter, Silence and Shouting: An Anthology of Women's Prayers*. Copyright © 1994. London: HarperCollins Publishers Limited, London.

Kierkegaard, Søren. Prayer #5491 ("For Courage to Hope") from *Søren Kierkegaard's Journals and Papers,* Volume 5 (p. 167). Edited and translated by Howard V. Hong and Edna H. Hong (Bloomington: Indiana University Press). Copyright © 1978 by Howard V. Hong. Permission granted by Indiana University Press.

Excerpt "The Apologist's Evening Prayer" by C. S. Lewis from *Poems by C. S. Lewis* edited by Walter Hooper. Copyright © 1964 by the Executors of the Estate of C. S. Lewis and renewed 1992 by C. S. Lewis Pte Ltd., reprinted by permission of Harcourt Brace and Company.

Excerpt from *The Prayers of Peter Marshall* edited by Catherine Marshall. Copyright © 1954 Fleming H. Revell.

Excerpt from *My God My Glory* by Eric Milner-White, re-issued 1994. Permission from Society for Promoting Christian Knowledge.

Excerpt "I Am More . . ." from *Praying with Jesus* by Eugene H. Peterson. Copyright © 1993 by Eugene H. Peterson. Reprinted by permission of HarperCollins Publishers, Inc.

Excerpt by Aleksandr Solzhenitsyn. Prayer translated by Patricia Blake. (*Time* magazine, April 3, 1972, p. 31.) Translation copyright © 1972. Used by permission of Patricia Blake.

Chapter 4

Excerpt from *Prayer in the Morning* by Jim Cotter. Copyright © 1989. Permssion to reprint granted by author.

147

Chapter 6

Index